Exceptional Monologues 2

for Men and Women

Edited by Roxane Heinze-Bradshaw
and Katherine DiSavino

A SAMUEL FRENCH ACTING EDITION

SAMUEL FRENCH

FOUNDED 1830

NEW YORK HOLLYWOOD LONDON TORONTO

SAMUELFRENCH.COM

ACKNOWLEDGEMENTS

Special thanks to Amy Rose Marsh, Kenneth Dingledine, Kellie Murphy, Nikki Jenkins, and Lauren Opper, who were all instrumental in the creation and development of this project.

A NOTE FROM THE EDITORS

Welcome to **Exceptional Monologues 2**! We are very pleased to be able to present you with these monologues, written by some of the most exciting playwrights on the scene today, including Itamar Moses, Sarah Ruhl, and Tina Howe, just to name a few. We think you'll be able to find valuable audition and class material within these pages, as well as a window into many of the new titles that we publish.

We've divided the book into Comedic and Dramatic, and from there, into Male and Female. Such black and white categorizations in genre don't always convey the complexities of a given monologue or play, but we've tried to gauge the overall mood of the chosen monologue in particular, independent of the play in which it appears. So be sure to look at the play synopsis provided to gain a better sense of the play as a whole.

In addition to a play synopsis, each monologue is provided with a scene synopsis, in order to help you contextualize the given selection and get into the character's head. Have some thoughts about the character's motivation? Why not jot them down in the notes section provided for your convenience with every piece. For a complete understanding of the play and your character's motivation, we suggest that you read the entire play as a part of your preparation to perform the monologue. For ordering information, visit our website at www.samuelfrench.com.

We've tried to place the monologues in ascending order of age range within each section, for ease of use. But don't let that stop you from browsing others! Also, if you flip to the back of the book, we've provided a thematic index as yet another tool in your search for the perfect-for-you monologue. And please note that although we have highlighted these particular monologues, there are many other monologues available, both in the plays selected for this collection and in our extensive catalogue, which we encourage you to seek out.

We certainly hope that this monologue collection might entice you to expand your theatrical horizons and explore the multifaceted world of contemporary playwriting. We think you will find it just as exceptional as we do!

Break a leg and keep your eyes open for further editions of the Samuel French Monologue and Scene Book series!

Roxane Heinze-Bradshaw, Editor &
Katherine DiSavino, Assistant Editor

CONTENTS

COMEDIC MONOLOGUES – MALE

COMEDIC MONOLOGUES – FEMALE

DRAMATIC MONOLOGUES – MALE

DRAMATIC MONOLOGUES – FEMALE

COMEDIC MONOLOGUES

MALE

End Days

Deborah Zoe Laufer

Play Synopsis: Sixteen year-old Rachel Stein is having a bad year. Her father hasn't changed out of his pajamas since 9/11. Her mother has begun a close, personal relationship with Jesus. Her new neighbor, a sixteen year-old Elvis impersonator, has fallen for her hard. And the Apocalypse is coming Wednesday. Her only hope is that Stephen Hawking will save them all.

Character: Nelson
Age: Teens
Genre: Comedic

Scene Synopsis: Nelson is new to the neighborhood and already has a crush on his neighbor, Rachel. When he meets her parents for the first time, he's so excited, he can hardly contain himself.

Notes:

THEMES: Love, Nerves, Adolescence

End Days

NELSON. My name. It's Nelson. Nelson Steinberg? It used to be Nelson Wallen, but then my step mom remarried and we changed our names and now it's Steinberg. Which is so great because I get to sit behind Rachel in homeroom. Stein. Steinberg? I also sit behind her in calculus. She's really great in math. Really great. Which is so wonderful for a girl. Not that girls are inherently poor in math, of course not, but, you know, sociological pressures make it uncommon for girls to excel in Math or Science. I bet she's great in science – wish I could sit behind her in science. Physics is amazing. They should start with physics in like kindergarten. Don't you think? Kids would really pay attention in math if they had physics earlier. I mean, it's like if they taught you to read before you could speak. You'd think, what are all these words, except you wouldn't think it in words, because you wouldn't know words yet. Did I just talk too much? Sometimes I do that. I'm supposed to look to see if anyone's interested but sometimes I forget to look, and sometimes even if I look it's hard to tell. People are really hard to read, don't you find? And then I get on a roll and it's hard for me to stop. I'm supposed to pretend to take an interest in the other person – ask questions so I don't monopolize the conversation, that's what they tell me. So…Tell me about yourself, Mr. S.

When Is A Clock

Matthew Freeman

Play Synopsis: When Gordon's wife vanishes, the only clue to her whereabouts is a bookmark in dog-eared copy of *Traveling to Montpelier*. With little help to be found at work, from his son, or from the police, Gordon takes off to a rural bookstore to find some answers. Through a fractured narrative that is half-mystery and half-memory, synchronicity, dreams, and alchemy combine in an exploration of what it means to be able to – and unable to – change.

Character: Alex
Age: Teens
Genre: Comedy

Scene Synopsis: Alex, unsure of where his mother has gone, and preoccupied with his teenage life, is unable to offer his father any information as to her whereabouts. Instead, he is only able to recount something that happened that afternoon at school.

Notes:

THEMES: SEX, RELIGION, ADOLESCENCE

When Is A Clock

ALEX. Jesus Christ. Jesus Motherfucking Christ. One of the nuns today went off. She just went insane. Fucking shit she went insane. Ok, ok, ok, so we're just standing outside and Sister Ashkelon comes out and tells us that Saint George had milk for blood. Ok, yes. Good. We're listening because we have no choice, right? Then she says that the dragon that Saint George supposedly slays actually represents a pagan cult. And that Saint George was a Roman who fought in Turkey. Ok, whatever. Why tell us all this, right? What's the fucking point?

(pause)

Then she, right, she starts to tell us that there's this rated R version of it. That basically the dragon was offered a princess as a human sacrifice because if she doesn't get fed to him, then they can't have water in this town for whatever reason. And it's like 2 A.D., right? So they can't think of things to do to fix it. So they're like, "Short straw, Princess. Down the dragon's gullet."

(pause)

So this soldier named George shows up from the Roman Army and he says, "You know what dragons dig? Tits." He takes off the Princess's bra, and then wraps it around the dragon's head and this whole thing hypnotizes the dragon and he winds up like, enchanted by her boob nets.

(pause)

Groovy. Then, right…this soldier leads the dragon back into town and what does he do? He totally shows off. He's like, "Take a gander, fellows and fellowladies. I am going to kill this totally zombified dragon, because I know how to handle a D cup." And then he kills the Dragon in the town square and everyone, I don't know, dances in its blood like Caligula and all that fun stuff. This is the story she tells us. This story about tits and stabbing stuff.

(pause)

Here's the obvious question: Should I whip it out for this nun? Because it appears as if she wants to get nailed.

THEMES: SEX, RELIGION, ADOLESCENCE

Back Back Back

Itamar Moses

Play Synopsis: Before headlines blazed, before the Mitchell Report and ESPN lit up millions of television screens with the scandals, before congressional jaws dropped, comes the story of three guys making their way in the world of professional baseball – a world too competitive to rely solely on raw talent...

Character: Raul
Age: 20s-30s
Genre: Comedic

Scene Synopsis: Raul, a baseball player, talks a little too freely to the press, as he is wont to do.

Notes:

Back Back Back

RAUL. I mean, it's complicated. But what I wish? Is I really wish more of the top guys had been able to see, you know, the link, between a salary cap and revenue sharing, by which I mean the practice of sharing revenue, which, combined with a cap on salaries, could have prevented this whole thing. But instead, we cut off the whole season and everybody in the whole country's feelings about the entire game of baseball are jeopardized because of just the greed that everybody exhibited through the whole thing. But you know what, guys? I think? A great player? Who is playing great? Could really help the game to bounce back from all this. But, see instead, with you guys, it's, you know, it's Bad Boy Raul is in town, and what kind of trouble is he gonna get into on the club, and what kind of shenanigans is he going to be involved in, and once again that's the story, and, frankly, I mean, I just, I find it kinda interesting, why a guy like me, or Barry, is the bad guy all the time, while another guy might not be the focus, and why that might be, instead of, oh, let's knock Raul again, because had some stupid injuries he could have avoided, or got hit on the head by a fly ball one time, or was maybe caught five years ago for speeding, or, whatever, crashing, because he was worked up from a fight he had with his wife at the time that, okay, maybe it got a little physical, but which was the whole reason he was speeding in the first place, and we've been divorced four years now, so leave it alone already, or who had a handgun one time in his car that the cops only even found because he left it on the seat after he accidentally, okay, accidentally parked in the handicapped spot at a hospital, which was the only reason they even looked, like it's not like I was even holding it! Because if that's the kind of thing that you guys want to write about, again, this year, instead of something positive? Then you guys go ahead and write about that. And I'll just know? In my heart? That that tells me a hell of a lot more about you guys than it says anything at all about me. Now if you'll excuse me I have a game to play.

Cockeyed
William Missouri Downs

Play Synopsis: Phil, an average nice guy, is madly in love with the beautiful Sophia. The only problem is that she's unaware of his existence. Perhaps he is caught in a philosophical hyperspace or dualistic reality or perhaps beautiful women are just unaware of nice guys. Armed only with a B.A. in philosophy, Phil sets out to prove his existence and win Sophia's heart.

Character: Phil
Age: 20s-30s
Genre: Comedic

Scene Synopsis: It's just another day at the office, when Phil loses himself in a fantasy about the woman he desperately loves from afar - his beautiful co-worker Sophia.

Notes:

THEMES: LOVE, FANTASY, LONGING

Cockeyed

PHIL. I've seen the woman I shall marry and she is without a doubt the most magnificent creature in all of New York – flawless except for one minor imperfection – she is totally unaware of my existence. There, through yonder door, 'tis the company break room and – Sophia. I've often daydreamed what our life together would be like. One day we'd accidentally meet in the break room and instantaneously click. There'd be no kiss on the first date; no, we'd both be too excited about our five-hour dialogue on Plato's allegory of the cave as it relates to the movie *The Matrix*. The first kiss would come on our second date – after a six hour heart-to-heart on Hitler and existentialism, I'd take her in my arms and with total confidence – something I've never known – I'd kiss her. A soft sigh would escape from her, letting me know that she had never been kissed like that before. On our wedding night we'd make love like Sartre and Simone de Beauvoir. After which, we'd lie in each other's arms and watch PBS or Book TV, or some other intellectually stimulating program. Kids? Lots. Marcus, René, Immanuel and the twins Jean-Paul and Ayn – all straight "A" students – except for Ayn, she's having trouble with Sartre's Essay on Phenomenological Ontology – but that's okay, she's only in the third grade. Then would come graduation day – Marcus, summa cum laude from Yale, René summa cum laude from Harvard, Immanuel, University of Michigan class valedictorian and the twins, Jean-Paul and Ayn, both Rhodes Scholars. And all of them philosophy majors – just like their father. And then one night, after a long evening with the family and extended family, I'd turn to Sophia and say "I think I'm a little tired." And we'd go upstairs. And make passionate love even though we're well into our nineties. After which, I'd lie in her arms. And the last words I'd hear would be "I love you sweetheart" as I drift off into a higher dimension, or non-existence, or whatever transcendental thing you wish to insert here. Aristotle says at the beginning of *Metaphysics*, "We take delight in our senses – apart from their usefulness they are loved for their own sake and none more than the sense of sight." I am in love with the sight of Sophia.

Fuente

Cusi Cram

Play Synopsis: Anything is possible in Fuente, an almost-real town, somewhere between where North America ends and South America begins. *Fuente* is a magically-real comedy set in a remote desert town about love, revenge, escape, and the perilous powers of Aqua Net hairspray.

Character: Chaparro
Age: 20s-30s
Genre: Comedic

Scene Synopsis: Chaparro defiantly extols the beauty and richness of his small desert town, Fuente, and the love he has for a woman from this town, named Soledad.

Notes:

THEMES: Desire, Love, Pride

Fuente

CHAPPARO. North of nowhere. South of bumfuck. East of your ass. Fuente. It gets all murky clear in my thinking. It's like the back of my hand and the back of Venus at once. Fuente. I say, I say to folks who ask, 'cause everybody thinks they got the right to know where you from. I say back at them, like they wanna hear, I say, Fuente. And they, with them grid-line, map charts of understanding up their fat asses, don't know where or what the fuck Fuente might be. I know. It is not a bedroom community. It is not a seaside resort. It's not Pleasantville or suburbia, or urban decay. It's not your city, village, or hamlet. It's not a crossroads or some spookety spook ghost town. It's not on map you can buy at your Exxon, 7-Eleven type establishment. It's not a locale, if you get my point. Fuente is Soledad. And she is un-mappable as a planet not yet discovered. She is the glass of lemonade with ice cubicles that you crave in high Fahrenheit heat. She is all things to anyone who wanted or knew wanting deep. She knows without asking and is mine, all mine. Mine. My mine. I mine her. I'm rich. So rich, I get silly. Silly in Fuente. Dry old Fuente. West of any thought you ever had. Soledad! Soledad!

THEMES: DESIRE, LOVE, PRIDE

For Better

Eric Coble

Play Synopsis: Karen and Max are getting married. At least, if their jobs will ever let them be in the same city at the same time. A romantic comedy for the digital age, *For Better* is a hilarious new farce that pokes fun at our overdependence on the gadgets in our lives.

Character: Stuart
Age: 30s
Genre: Comedic

Scene Synopsis: Stuart, crashing the wedding of a long-time friend to tell the bride he loves her, nervously chats with the bride-to-be's father.

Notes:

For Better

STUART. My strongest memory of flowers was this family trip we took when I was eight, out to visit my aunt in Vermont. And as we drove we passed this field. I mean a huge field, acres and acres of wildflowers, and not just one kind of wildflower, you know where one species pretty much commits flower genocide and wipes out every competing flower, no, there were dozens, two dozen, three dozen kinds of flowers – every color, every shape as far as the eye could see. And my father pulled over. Which was something considering we usually got one bathroom break per state – which gave us a keen sense of geography, let me tell you – Kansas is a very, very wide state it turns out – but we all just got out of the car – wordlessly, which was also something of first in my clan, and we just stood there staring at this ocean of color and texture. Unfortunately, my mother insisted we go lie down in the flowers so she could get a picture, and we did, and it turns out not only was this a magical place for us, but was the single greatest magnet for honey bees in the tri-state region. We arrived at my aunt's house approximately three times the size we left our house. So I have mixed feelings about flowers. But these are lovely! These should stay!

THEMES: FAMILY, MEMORY, FLOWERS

The 39 Steps

Patrick Barlow

Play Synopsis: Mix a Hitchcock masterpiece with a juicy spy novel, add a dash of Monty Python and you have *The 39 Steps*, a fast-paced whodunit for anyone who loves the magic of theatre! This 2-time Tony® and Drama Desk Award-winning treat is packed with nonstop laughs, over 150 zany characters (played by a cast of 4), an on stage plane crash, handcuffs, missing fingers and some good old-fashioned romance!

Character: Hannay
Age: 30s-40s
Genre: Comedic

Scene Synopsis: Hannay, on the run from the police, finds himself being confused for a politician at a rally. He's called to the podium to give the key-note address and finds inspiration from his current predicament.

Notes:

The 39 Steps

HANNAY. Thanks awfully. Well I've been pretty busy all my life really. Well actually not recently. Recently I've been in a bit of a slump to be honest. Catching myself in the lonely hours, full of damned – thoughts and what have you. Well not that recently. Recently, the last few days – well the last day really, everything's gone a bit haywire frankly. Wouldn't say it's been easy. Pretty damned difficult actually. But the odd thing is – the odd thing is – you carry on! And it's pretty bracing when you do. Pulls a chap out of himself if you know what I mean. There he is. No idea what's happening. Who to trust. Where to turn. Whether it'll be worth it at the end of it all. But something – I don't know – stirs the old bones! Gets the old ticker pumping again! And there's no time to think. And your mind's singing. And your heart's racing. And you're meeting people. Real people! Doing the best they can! Yes! Doing the best they can in all the terrible situations the world throws at them! Suffering things no man or woman ought to suffer! And yet they carry on! They don't give up! They damn well keep going! And I'll tell you what else they do. They do the best they can for other people too! Whatever problems they've got, they damn well look after each other! Is that such an outmoded sentimental notion? Is it!? Well is it? So look here – let's just all set ourselves resolutely to make this world a happier place! A decent world! A good world! A world where no nation plots against nation! Where no neighbour plots against neighbour, where there's no persecution or hunting down, where everybody gets a square deal and a sporting chance and where people try to help and not to hinder! A world where suspicion and cruelty and fear have been forever banished! So I'm asking you – each and every one of you here tonight –

(He points at members of the audience.)

you and you and – and – definitely you! Is that the sort of world you want? Because that's the sort of world I want! What do you think? Let's vote on it! Come on! Vote for a good world! A better world! A new world! And above all – vote for Mr. McCrocodile! There! That's all I have to say. Thank you.

THEMES: PERSEVERANCE, SACRIFICE, COURAGE

Aliens With Extraordinary Skills

Saviana Stanescu

Play Synopsis: A dark comedy about a clown from the "unhappiest country in the world," Moldova, who pins her hopes on a US work visa. Chased by Homeland Security, a deportation letter deflates Nadia's enthusiasm and a pair of spike heels might be all it takes to burst her American Dream – or turn it into a nightmare...

Character: Bob
Age: 30s
Genre: Comedic

Scene Synopsis: Bob, slightly tipsy and at the urging of a new friend, retells the story of what he recently told his psychiatrist.

Notes:

Aliens With Extraordinary Skills

BOB. OK. So…I went to my shrink last week, she's this upscale woman in her 50s…And she's like, "Why do you date women whose mother tongue is not English, Bob?" And I'm like: You're a shrink, haven't you noticed? When you are forced to pay closer attention to people's words, you actually communicate better. If you both speak English and you both think you know what you're talking about, there's all this room for misinterpretation about what's actually being said. But if you are not sure that the other person is getting you, you check her out, you make sure she gets you. And if…if she's not sure she's getting you, she checks you out, you know, she pays attention, until she gets you…And even the silences begin to have some meaning, you know, because you're used to paying attention to each other…On my tours with the band, we had groupies, fans, all that. We traveled abroad: Mexico, Eastern Europe, Russia…And believe me, those girls were really paying attention to us. Not just as musicians: as men, as people…Then I married this waspy Upper West Side girl and everything fucking changed. She got me a office job at her dad's company. I tried to talk to her. In our mutual language – English. Did she get what I said? No. Nothing. Nada. Look at me now. I don't go on tours anymore. My pals gave up on me. I stopped playing music when I became that shitty office rat…Of course she kicked me out of the apartment. Had a better lawyer. And you know what, as fucked up as that may sound, I'm OK with this new situation. I don't wanna do anything for a while. Just… live. Gimme a bunch of beers to keep me company and I'm happy these days. I got this cool little job at Video&Music Rentals. I'm doing my little thing…And you know something else, I said: I can't afford these therapy sessions. You take less than my last shrink, but still…I'm outta here. It was only 7 minutes, wasn't it? Twenty bucks should do it. Cheers! To foreign women!

What They Have
Kate Robin

Play Synopsis: Connie and Jonas are a successful industry couple. Their friends Suzanne, a struggling painter, and Matt, a struggling musician, can't afford to fix the roof. But stay tuned because in this funny, poignant, and always truthful play, lives can change in a heartbeat, and things aren't necessarily what they seem.

Character: Matt
Age: 30s
Genre: Comedic

Scene Synopsis: Matt is growing tired of the lives parents must lead, and he shares his frustration with a close friend.

Notes:

What They Have

MATT. Don't all the grown-ups seem really...depressing? I mean, have you been to a playground, lately? All the parents. They look like total shit, man. And they have nothing to say. When you try to talk to them, they tell you how many hours their kid slept last night. And the night before. And the night before that. Like that's a conversation. And they all have these deranged looks in their eye. Screaming, "Good job! Good job!" every time the kid comes down the slide, or drinks from his stupid sippy cup. And dude, the words that come out of your mouth – "binky?" "burpie?" "diapie?" "She had a big poopy!" That's, like, the most dramatic event of my day. My mom used to always say, "It's different when they're yours," but I can see these parents are bored out of their minds. They're in a coma, man. And so was my mother, actually. It wasn't different for her. She had to be on barbiturates to make it through a day at the park. *(pause)* And everyone spends their whole pregnancy coming up with a perfect retro name, like that's going to make the whole family incredibly cool, and then it turns out we all came up with same five names. Suzanne almost lost her mind when she found out how many Ellas there are in our neighborhood. She went to this New Mother's group, which is another place you should avoid if you ever want to have an erection again in your life, and there were like six hundred baby Ellas. I thought she was going to just gun them all down.

Men of Tortuga

Jason Wells

Play Synopsis: Four men conspire to defeat a despised opponent by a ruthless act of violence: they will fire a missile into a crowded conference room on the day of an important meeting. Maxwell, a hero of the old guard, volunteers to sacrifice himself for the plan, but things become more complicated as Maxwell grows close to one of the men who will be collatoral damage if their plan is carried through.

Character: Taggart
Age: 30s
Genre: Comedic

Scene Synopsis: An assassin reasons with a group of men who have only one target in mind. The logistics of the hit are near-impossible to carry out, and it seems like the only option is to evaluate whether more drastic measures, resulting in more casualties, is worth ensuring that their target dies.

Notes:

THEMES: CHOICE, SACRIFICE, DEATH

Men of Tortuga

TAGGART. Okay. You want to kill a man. You want to cause as little
collateral damage as possible. Of course. "As possible" is the
key. So the question becomes, how much do you care? What
is the cost of each life, compared to the reward of success? It
becomes a question of statistics. Say you're on the battlefield
and you just want to kill one general. If you could pick him off
with a rifle, you would, and that would be that. You have nothing against his soldiers. Everyone goes home. But you can't
get him like that, so you turn to your array of weapons, and
what do you have? Cannons. You can't hope to kill one man
with a cannonball. The idea of a cannonball is to fire it into
a crowd of enemies and see what it does. It takes this guy's
head off, knocks that guy's arm off, bounces around, breaks
another guy's leg. You don't care which guys; it's a weapon of
general destruction. It's addressed to "Occupant." "To whom
it may concern," right? You're working with statistics. Now
somebody figured out that you could improve a cannonball
by filling it with gunpowder and lighting the fuse before you
fire it. Now it takes out two or three guys, then it blows up and
kills three more. Now what if you had enough cannonballs to
kill everyone? Or better yet, one giant cannonball that kills
everyone in one shot. You would get your man, wouldn't you?
Your one man. But before you do it, you have that question:
"Do I want him that bad? Or can I let him live so that these
others may live?"

Folks: This can be done. You just have to want to do it.

In the Sawtooths

Dano Madden

Play Synopsis: Oby, Nellie, and Darin have been friends since high school. Now in their thirties, they have become busier in their lives, but one thing remains constant: their annual backpacking adventure. As their trip nears, their lives are suddenly shattered by tragedy. What ensues is a true test of an old friendship. Can they remain friends as they desperately try to navigate through an immense and unexpected wilderness?

Character: Nellie
Age: 30s
Genre: Comedic

Scene Synopsis: On a camping trip, Nellie tells his buddies a story of how he romanced his friend, Sara, in the great outdoors, under the influence of campfire and s'mores.

Notes:

In the Sawtooths

NELLIE. I took Sara Summers up to Loon Lake a few years ago. She had never been hiking before and she loved the scenery and the hike, unlike Lisa. We had a very romantic dinner by the fire and then I suggested that we make s'mores for dessert. Sara had never heard of s'mores. So. I said, "Sara, what a shame. Allow me to enlighten you." I broke off a piece of dark chocolate. Marshmallow toasted to perfection. I was born with that ability. Born with it. *(beat)* I then put the graham crackers, chocolate and a marshmallow together and – Up to this point, I should probably note, Sara Summers and I were only friends. I had never even kissed her. So, I gave Sara the s'more, and, I, it's difficult to explain how she took a bite, but it caused me physical pain. Her lips, the light of the fire on her face. Those eyes. My God. Those brown eyes. She then offered me a bite. But instead of handing me the s'more, she fed it to me. Wiping crumbs from my mouth with her fingers. Let's just say that was the beginning of a very good camping trip. My kind of adventure.

THEMES: LOVE, ROMANCE, DISCOVERY

Skin Deep
Jon Lonoff

Play Synopsis: In *Skin Deep*, a large, lovable, lonely-heart named Maureen Mulligan, gives romance one last shot on a blind-date with sweet, awkward Joseph Spinelli; she's learned to pepper her speech with jokes to hide insecurities about her weight and appearance, while he's almost dangerously forthright, saying everything that comes to his mind. They both know they're perfect for each other, and in time they come to admit it.

Character: Joe Spinelli
Age: 40s
Genre: Comedic

Scene Synopsis: On his first date with Maureen, Joe opens up about his frustration over being single when all of his siblings have spouses and children. He knows that by not taking action, he's let chances at love go by. But has he learned from his mistakes?

Notes:

THEMES: LOVE, LONELINESS, ADOLESCENCE

Skin Deep

JOE. My pop used to say that a guy gets three shots at marriage: when he's young and good-looking; when he's middle-aged and well-off; when he's old and the only thing left standing. I figure if I can hang on for another twenty years I'll make out okay. My pop used to say I'm one of those "Nice Guys who Finish Last." But as long as I finish, right? *(laughs)* I remember my first little girlfriend, from Dyker Heights Junior High School 201. Francine Tetarian. Franny. This was a girl who never talked to anyone; the other kids made fun of her frizzy hair; she was thin as a dime; she had teeth so crooked, kids would pay to watch her eat lunch; and she always smelled like a boiled frankfurter. And I was crazy about her. One day, at the bus stop, I stepped in front of "Big Donny Battigliani" who was yankin' at her books. I shoved Donny on the ground and held him down until he apologized and ran away. Everyday after that...I was her hero. I waited with Francine for the bus. And in 8th grade, *(mock tough)* there's nothin' – but nothin' – more manly than protectin' your woman at a bus stop. One day, right before she climbed onto the bus, she turned to me, closed her little eyes and stuck out her lips.

But I just stood there. *(pause)* So she got on the bus and the bus rolled away. *(laughs at himself)* Weeks later, I figured it out: she wanted me to kiss her! But by that time, she was going steady with "Big Donny Battigliani." Yeah. *(shrugs off)* That was the first of a lotta chances I let go by. A lotta chances. Like filling up a bingo card and not yelling bingo. *(a small laugh, then)* So why aren't you married? What's your problem?

THEMES: LOVE, LONELINESS, ADOLESCENCE

Apostasy
Gino DiIorio

Play Synopsis: Sheila Gold, fity-five, a successful Jewish businesswoman suffering from terminal cancer, is spending the end of her life in a comfortable hospice where her only companion is her thirty year-old daughter, Rachel. When Sheila becomes fascinated with a late night televangelist, Dr. Julius Strong, and writes to tell him that she will make a sizable donation to his ministry, he flies out to visit her, and the two fall in love. But is it true love, or is the good minister just out for Rachel's inheritance?

Character: Julius
Age: 50s
Genre: Comedic

Scene Synopsis: Julius entertains Sheila, claiming he can testify on any subject. She suggests "McDonalds."

Notes:

THEMES: SPONTANEITY, RELIGION, HAPPINESS

Apostasy

JULIUS. McDonald's Food.

(He stands on the chair and grabs a Bible.)

I was standing in line, waiting on the line, like so many others, just waiting to be served, waiting to be nourished, waiting to place an order so my soul would be fulfilled. And I said, I would like to order some chicken McNuggets, please. Now, I didn't say I wanted to order any four piece. No, no, no. I said, I'd like the six piece; with some extra dipping sauce. Because I deserve it, don't you know. And I took my paper bag, and I was ready to accept the good grace of the Lord, and accept these six…nuggets of…what part of the chicken they are, I do not know. But there they were, just waiting for me and I sat down and just like that I realized I was lost, brothers and sisters. For I realized in my haste, I had forgotten to take myself some extra dipping sauce. I had no honey mustard. I had no spicy barbecue. It was nowhere to be found. I was at wit's end, the end of my rope. I would have to somehow manage with these poor, lonely, six chicken McNuggets, without a dipping sauce to dip them in. I was just about to give up, when sitting there on the bench, the McDonald Land bench, all alone, just me and my happy meal, I looked inside the bag, and there it was, sitting in the corner, like hope at the bottom of Pandora's box, one genuine container of dipping sauce. My searching was over. It was always there, brothers and sisters. Down in the very bottom of the bag they call life. Don't be searching for happiness, let happiness come to you. And remember to ask the girl for the sauce before you leave the counter. Praise God.

THEMES: SPONTANEITY, RELIGION, HAPPINESS

Easter Monday
Hal Corley

Play Synopsis: An eccentric widower, Mack has been a stay-at-home dad for twenty years, his daily existence revolving around his son Billy. Not only can't he let go, on the contrary – Mack's convinced he's more needed than ever.

Character: Mack
Age: 50s
Genre: Dramatic

Scene Synopsis: Mack, slightly panicky when discovering that his adopted son has been in touch with his birth mother, tells him about the night he and his wife brought him back to New York on the train from Washington DC, after the adoption.

Notes:

THEMES: FAMILY, LOVE, BELONGING

Easter Monday

MACK. 'Night we brought you home, it was October. Leaves had turned, but it was so sticky. 'Cause it was Columbus Day, we had to come back from Washington on the slow train, and the air conditionin' was on the fritz, and there weren't enough seats. So I stood part of the way, and my whole shirt got sopping wet. Then black, from this dirt n'soot coming in the window. Mommy's whirlin' dervish mind started thinking about all the darn troubles on the horizon. Would this dark little place still be big enough for us all. Could we send ya to PS 87. Would her job at the bank be there when she was ready to go back – Yeah, well, she was ready in a month. All her worrying gave me a migraine, so I sent her off to the dining car. While Mommy was buyin' herself two so-called light beers and a ham sandwich, I changed my first diaper. I guess nobody on that slow train had ever seen a man touch a diaper before, 'cause everybody was whisperin' and pointing and smiling. When somebody pulled out their camera and took a picture of me, a coupla people clapped. I felt famous, like I'd just found the Lindbergh baby.

(beat)

And...relieved. For the first time, I knew what I was born to do.

Shtick

Henry Meyerson

Play Synopsis: Helen's life becomes complicated when her husband, Murray, has a stroke and her younger sister, Gladys, reveals that she and Murray had been having an affair. Helen suspected Murray was no angel when she married him, and while Helen might have been willing to adjust to Murray and his new stroke-induced limits, the stakes are raised by Gladys's admission of the affair.

Character: Murray
Age: 60s
Genre: Comedic

Scene Synopsis: Murray returns home where his wife, Helen, and her sister, Gladys, are waiting. Usually quite the comic, Murray explains his previously unstated feelings to Helen.

Notes:

Shtick

MURRAY. Just listen. See, I'm sitting in this Starbucks, working on this new routine, but I'm also watching all the young ass go by and I'm getting an erection. I swear. It was amazing. Well, not so amazing. In fact, it wasn't much of an erection, but it was a beginning. Anyway I'm sitting there as stunned as you two are about what's happening, when it suddenly occurs to me that even though I got this thing going on in my head and my pants, these young girls didn't give a shit if I lived or died. To them I'm just an old piece of meat waiting to die. Then I think, so what am I doing here. I should be going home. But then I suddenly remembered something else and this sealed it. Helen, you were right this morning. You said I never told you I loved you. And you were right. All these years, I never told you I loved you. Remember what you told me this morning, Helen? Knowing what you know now, hating what I did, feeding me coffee because I couldn't hold the cup, having to cut my meat, feed me, take me to the toilet, dress me, a sex life that's a memory, despite all of that having to be my caretaker. That's what you said, Helen. And then I had the balls to ask you if you loved me. So what I came to realize in that Starbucks was that in addition to everything else that's wrong with me, I'm also a stupid, old man. I love you, Helen. I've always loved you. Despite my selfishness, I always loved you and I always will. That's what I discovered. And I'm not saying that because I need you. I'm saying that because I want you.

THEMES: LOVE, FAMILY, AGING

Dead Man's Cell Phone
Sarah Ruhl

Play Synopsis: An incessantly ringing cell phone in a quiet café. A stranger at the next table who has had enough. And a dead man – with a lot of loose ends. *Dead Man's Cell Phone* is a work about how we memorialize the dead – and how that remembering changes us.

Character: Gordon
Age: 30s-40s
Genre: Comedic

Scene Synopsis: Gordon recalls the last moments of his life, reflecting on his choices and struggling to make sense of it all.

Notes:

Dead Man's Cell Phone

GORDON. But that day – the day I died – I didn't want to eat something that reminded me of body parts. I woke up in the morning wanting a lobster bisque. So I get off the subway, go to the cafe, the place I always go. A familiar guy behind the counter, a giant, with really huge knuckles. I said, I'll have the lobster bisque. He said, sorry we're out, as though it was a casual, everyday thing to be out of lobster bisque on the day I was going to die, as though I could come back the following week. As though it were a friendly, careless matter – sorry, we're out.

So I said: did you have any ten minutes ago?

And the giant said, yes.

I said, is anyone at this restaurant currently eating a lobster bisque?

And the giant said, well yes.

Who?

And he pointed to a woman in the corner. A pale-ish woman, sort of non-descript.

So I say, I will purchase her bowl of soup.

What? He says. I take out my wallet, pull out a hundred.

Then I see it – she is tilting the bowl to the side to scrape out the last bite.

I watch it go into her little mouth, slow motion.

Son of a bitch, I say. I'll have lentil.

I'm used to getting what I want. But today is not my day. So I have the lentil.

Lentil soup is never that great. It's only ever serviceable. It doesn't really make your mouth water, does it, lentil soup? Something watery – something brown – and hot carrots. Like death. Serviceable, a little mushy and warm in the wrong places, not as bad as you'd think it's going to be, not as good, either. Suddenly I feel my heart – compressing – like a terrible bird in my chest. And I think – I'm finally punished. Someone is going to sell my heart to someone in Russia. Then I think – use your cell phone. Call your wife. Tell her to give you a

THEMES: DESIRE, DEATH, FORGIVENESS

decent burial, organs in tact. But the wife's not supposed to know you sell organs for a living. So just call the wife and say good-bye. But no – she doesn't love you enough to have the right tone of voice on your death bed. The kind of voice you'd like to hear – indescribably tender. A death-bed voice.

Gordon having a heart-attack, heaving.

No longer holding it in – the things people hold back from each other – whole lives – most people give in at the last moment – but not Hermia, no – she'll be sealed up – she'll keep a little bit extra for herself – that last nugget of pride – she'll reserve it for her tin can spine – so she'll have an extra half inch of height. That thing – that wedge, that cold wedge between – I can't call her. No. A disappointment. So call your mistress. Or mother. No – mother would say – what a way to die, Gordon, in a café? No, not mother. Dwight? A man doesn't call his brother on his death-bed – no – he wants a woman's voice – But the heart keeps on heaving itself up – out of my chest – into my mouth – and I'm thinking – that bitch over there ate all the lobster bisque, this is all her fault – and I look over at her, and she looks like an angel – not like a bitch at all – and I think – good – good – I'm glad she had the last bite – I'm glad.

Then I die.

COMEDIC MONOLOGUES

FEMALE

Wedding Belles

Alan Bailey and Ronnie Claire Edwards

Play Synopsis: Four garden-club ladies meet a young girl who has come to their little Texas town to marry an infantryman before he ships off for World War II. The women impulsively decide to throw the girl an elaborate wedding, and their lives and friendships are thrown into turmoil as they race to accomplish the nuptials in one frenzied afternoon.

Character: Ima Jean
Age: Teens
Genre: Comedic

Scene Synopsis: Ima Jean tells the ladies about her adventures on the bus from Oklahoma, and why she is so hungry.

Notes:

Wedding Belles

IMA JEAN. I fried me up a baloney sandwich last night for the trip, but I made myself only eat half of it. And I had a Mason jar of lemonade to wash it down. But the bus driver swerved – I think he was purposely trying to hit a big ol' armadillo in the road – and that lemonade sloshed all over me and the sack I had my sandwich in. When I fished it out, it wasn't too drownded, so I wrapped it up in my handkerchief and set it on the seat beside me. I nodded off and I reckon it was about three-thirty or four when I woke up and I was kindly famished. So I turned to get my sandwich – and now, you won't believe this part – there was a big ol' fat man sitting where my sandwich used to be. Just a teensy bit of my handkerchief peeking out from under them great big rolls of fat. And I thought, "Oh Lordy, what am I going to do?" He was gone to the world. But you know, hunger does funny things to a person. I had to accept the fact that if I wanted that sandwich, I was going to have to fight for it. Never in my wildest dreams did I imagine I would ever touch that man's fat, but I eased my hand up under there – first one roll – then another – then another – and I lifted. Now you won't believe this part – my sandwich had fallen into the space between the two seats! It was wedged in there tighter than a tick. It was safe! So with one hand, I kept that fat lifted up and with the other, I ever so gently eased my sandwich out. And just as I got it, the bus pulls into a station and the fat man wakes up with a big snort. Starts flailing his arms around. Knocked the sandwich right out of my hand. But then the driver opens the door and the floor lights come on. And I seen it. There it was, away up front. And now, you won't believe this part – my handkerchief was nowhere to be seen. My sandwich was laying there nekkid on the bus floor. And just as I'm creeping up there for it, here comes a blind man with a big ol' dog, scarfed it right down. So yes, ma'am, I'm a mite hungry.

Up

Bridget Carpenter

Play Synopsis: *Up* invites us into the life of Walter Griffin, a failed inventor obsessed with Philippe Petit's famed 1974 wire-walk between the twin World Trade Center towers. Walter's greatest moment of glory – a flight on a lawn chair festooned with helium balloons – is now long behind him, though Walter dreams of inventing something wonderful once more.

Character: Maria
Age: Teens
Genre: Comedic

Scene Synopsis: Maria, a pregnant teen, is new to Mikey's school, and senses a kindred spirit in him the first time they meet. She has no qualms about opening up.

Notes:

THEMES: FAMILY, CHANGE, ADOLESCENCE

Up

MARIA. I've seen the girls around here. Snotty, right? Those kind of girls always want to call some shitbag football player their "boyfriend." Kinda guy who'll take you out, get tanked on keg beer playing quarters, then try to shove his hand up your shirt. Pathetic. You shouldn't worry about it too much. Not having a girlfriend I mean. Anybody who peaks in high school is a dismal failure, bound to be on a downward spiral for the rest of their lives. That's what my aunt says, anyway. She says that high school is the worst fucking mess anyone ever has to endure, and that every job that follows is socially simpler, so I'm just waiting it out, you know? I live with my Aunt Chris. My mom tried to kick me out when she found out I was gonna have the sprout. The pitter-patter of little feet would have put a cramp into her booze time. Aunt Chris called my mom a drunk bitch with no sense of responsibility and she said I could move in with her. So I did. Week after I got there, we moved to Sacramento. Me and my mom used to live in Venice in a shithole but it was cool to be near the beach. My aunt's work takes her all over, that's why we went to Sacramento. I've been all over California: Fresno, Temecula, San Diego, San Dimas, Santa Maria, Riverside this is a big state.

(beat)

I just change schools when we move. Swing with the changes, that's what my aunt says. That's why this dump doesn't faze me.

You don't talk much, do you?

THEMES: FAMILY, CHANGE, ADOLESCENCE

Fuente
Cusi Cram

Play Synopsis: Anything is possible in Fuente, an almost-real town, somewhere between where North America ends and South America begins. *Fuente* is a magically-real comedy set in a remote desert town about love, revenge, escape, and the perilous powers of Aqua Net hairspray.

Character: Blair-Maria
Age: Teens
Genre: Comedic

Scene Synopsis: Blair-Maria has magic in her she doesn't understand. Magic that makes her float. Suspended in mid-air, unable to descend, she carries out a conversation with Jesus, talking directly to a crucifix that hangs on her bedroom wall.

Notes:

THEMES: RELIGION, ADOLESCENCE, FRUSTRATION

Fuente

BLAIR-MARIA. I take it back. I'm not sorry. Asswipe. Cocksucker. Motherfucker. *(a beat)* I wasn't saying those things about you, just in front of you. It's not like you ever stop me. *(a moment)* How come you never move your lips? Or cry? Or burp, even? It's always me blabbing away and you quieter than Fuente on a Sunday night. I got some BONES to pick with you. A whole platter of them. First bone: when you can take a minute from your busy schedule, I'd really like to get down from here. This some kind a joke to you? Some weirdass prank? I got two words for you: not funny. Another bone: why'd you go and make my Daddy blind? I know he might not believe in you exactly but he believes in some kinda God and never says an unkind word about anyone and that should count for something. Huge bone – this is the biggest one buddy – you got some kind of crazy nerve to give me the frizzies two nights before prom. I am known in three counties for my perfect hair. And nothing, not even special gels from the expensive hairdresser up in Oriba, would make the frizz go away. I even went into Mamá's closet and sprayed some old fashioned hair spray, the kind old ladies wear, the kind that could protect your head from a tornado. I think it's called Aquaknit. It has strange foreign writing on the label. But it don't matter what it's called, my head still looks like a Brillo pad. Thanks for that, big time. Another thing, it's not a bone exactly but a serious complaint: we need a bar in Fuente, OK?. As it stands now, we gotta drive fifty miles to Catena for a cocktail. Most kids just buy beer at the 7 Eleven with their fake ID's but since Mamá owns every 7-Eleven in two hundred miles, she went and gave pictures to all of her clerks of me and my friends, I can't even buy one of them O'Doull fake beers. Drives Tommy nuts. And I don't even like beer. *(Alexis Carrington voice)* Tequila's my particular poison, darling. *(Blair -Maria is not quite sure where those words came from.)* I only had it once but it was it was a good time until it wasn't. Tommy promised to get three bottles for prom from the package store in Lost River. Now that's love. That's almost three hours round trip. That's Tommy. Why am I wasting my breath on you, anyway? You can't hear me. It's like you gotta a head cold. A permanent one.

Out of Sterno

Deborah Zoe Laufer

Play Synopsis: Dotty's life in Sterno with her husband Hamel is absolutely perfect! It's a fairy tale, it really is. True, in their seven years of marriage Hamel has forbidden her to leave their tiny apartment or speak to anyone, but Dotty is so very happy to spend her days watching video re-enactments of the day they first met. When a phone call from a mysterious woman threatens to tear her world asunder, Dotty must venture out into the vast city of Sterno, and try to discover what it is to be a "real" woman.

Character: Dottie
Age: 20s
Genre: Comedic

Scene Synopsis: Dottie decides to take a moment to tell the audience a little bit about her beloved husband, revealing much more about her life than even she realizes.

Notes:

Out of Sterno

DOTTY. First time I laid eyes on Hamel, I passed right out. He's got that kind of charisma. I was sixteen. He moved to our town from someplace else. No one had ever done that before so there was a lot of commotion. Every time I heard about him, I could feel my ears get hot. Then June 3rd, 2:30 p.m., I was at Joyner's store getting myself a chocolate Yoohoo and in walks Hamel. He looks me over, does this *(click click)* with the side of his teeth and says,"Hey, kid." Well. When I came to, I see Hamel standing over me. He goes – *(She whistles.)* "What a nut!" And a week later we were married! Now we live in Sterno, which is a huge huge city, and Hamel works at the Mobil oil station, and we're so much in love! It's like a fairytale, it really is. I don't exactly know anyone here, yet. Hamel doesn't much like for me to talk with other people. He's so crazy about me he wants me all to himself! I love that. I bet it took a while for my mama to get used to never seeing or talking to me but like she always said, "Make your man the center of your world and you'll never get lost." I haven't actually ever even left this apartment! Not since we moved in seven years ago.

(reacting to the audience)

No, no – that's a-ok with me. This is just about the greatest place on earth! All this and at six fifteen sharp, Hamel himself.

(looks at a kitchen clock)

Four minutes to Hamel time! So any of you ladies who are prone to fainting, get out your smelling salts!

THEMES: MARRIAGE, LOVE, CONTROL

The Divine Fallacy
from Shrinking Violets and Towering Tiger Lilies

Tina Howe

Play Synopsis: A camera-shy novelist needs a headshot for her upcoming novel. Chaos ensues during her photo shoot with a suave fashion photographer.

Character: Dorothy
Age: 20s-30s
Genre: Comedic

Scene Synopsis: Dorothy desperately tries to explain to her photographer her feelings of inadequacy in front of the camera.

Notes:

The Divine Fallacy

DOROTHY. This was her idea, not mine! I hate having my picture taken! *(struggling to get past him)* I hate it, hate it, hate it, hate it, hate it, hate it, hate it, hate it... *Hate it, hate it, hate it, hate it!* Why can't you set up your camera in my brain? Bore a hole in my skull and let 'er rip. *(She makes lurid sound effects.)* There's no plainness here, but heaving oceans ringed with pearls and ancient cities rising in the mist... Grab your tripod and activate your zoom, wonders are at hand... Holy men calling the faithful to prayer as women shed their clothes at the river's edge... Click! Jeweled elephants drink beside them, their trunks shattering the surface like breaking glass. Click! Their reflections shiver and merge, woman and elephant becoming one... Slender arms dissolving into rippling tusks, loosened hair spreading into shuddering flanks... Click, click, click! Now you see them, now you don't A breast, a tail, a winking eye... Click! Macaws scream over head *(sound effect)*, or is it the laughter of the women as they drift further and further from the shore, their shouts becoming hoarse and strange... *(sound effect)* Click! *(tapping her temple)* Aim your camera here, Mr. Hugo. This is where beauty lies... Mysterious, inchoate and out of sight! *(suddenly depressed)* I don't know about you, but I could use a drink.

THEMES: BEAUTY, FEAR, ANXIETY

Ayravana Flies, or A Pretty Dish
from Off Off Broadway Festival Plays, 33rd Series

Sheila Callaghan

Play Synopsis: Olivia is a frizzy-haired nutty-looking waitress with too-red lipstick and bulgy omnivorous eyes. Elephant is a reticent, dapper pachyderm in a business suit. He orders the Special of the Day. One heimlich maneuver plus a taste for the exotic equals love. Or dinner.

Character: Olivia
Age: 20s-30s
Genre: Comedic

Scene Synopsis: Olivia exults in the rediscovery of a lost talent: cooking.

Notes:

Ayravana Flies, or A Pretty Dish

OLIVIA. SO. Chop chop chop I go, dice dice dice chop, mix mix, taste, mix mix sprinkle sprinkle pour, mix mix taste, cook cook cook cook cook taste sprinkle cook cook cook cook taste scream swear, cook cook cook cook cook cook taste and smile. And I'm shuttled to another time and place, growing up as a little girl on the vegetable farm. No. Yes, the vegetable farm. In my Tom Sawyer overalls and my straw hat and my bare feet, skipping through the plantation and digging up vegetables from the warm soil, then skipping home with a full basket and cooking them all up in a big wicker pot, then adding special spices I'd ordered from my spice catalogue, exotic spices with names too long to pronounce, from countries too small to see, and I'd serve them warm in a loaf of bread with the heart torn out. Oooooooh. Mmmmmmm. La la la la la. People clamored at my kitchen window in frenzied hordes for a taste of my wildly original dishes. "Olivia is cooking in her wicker pot again, bring the tin foil and the toothpicks!" Tearing each other's hair, ripping their own shirts. For a TASTE, I tell you. And after one bite they'd drop to the dirt in a swoon. Because I made more than just dishes. I made VOODOO. Not the creepy kind with the mumbling and the eyes-rolled back and the rag doll stuck with pins. The good kind. I burned flavors into peoples mouth – memories. I could conjure music from the tip of the tongue to the uvula, each tiny increment of space resounding a different chord. It was clear I had a future as a Voodoo Priestess of Culinary Wizardry. But alas. I got thwarted somewhere between point A and point A. Until now.

For Better

Eric Coble

Play Synopsis: Karen and Max are getting married. At least, if their jobs will ever let them be in the same city at the same time. A romantic comedy for the digital age, *For Better* is a hilarious new farce that pokes fun at our overdependence on the gadgets in our lives.

Character: Karen
Age: 30s
Genre: Comedic

Scene Synopsis: Karen's father wants to watch his television programs, but Karen has some big (and unexpected) news for him.

Notes:

For Better

KAREN. I'm getting married, Dad. Is it great? It's great, isn't it? We just met – not just met, we met at the International Retail Foods Conference in Tampa last year and we've only seen each other twice since then, but we talk everyday – multiple times everyday – I haven't actually seen him in two months but he asked me to marry him! He proposed! Which is so like him once you get to know him – he just does it, he thinks, he does it – everyone else in food management is so "stay with the itinerary," "stick to the Power Point," but he's all instinct, and his instinct was to fall in love and mine was too and his instinct was to propose and mine was to accept, I think, I mean, I think it's okay, right, and he's calling you to ask for my hand in marriage, your permission – He's very old-fashioned. Impulsive and old-fashioned. Be nice to him, please be nice to him!

Fatboy
John Clancy

Play Synopsis: *Fatboy* is a brutal comedy inspired by Alfred Jarry's *Ubu Roi*. This satire on modern America's insatiable appetites – from gobbling up 72oz. steaks to small nations – is presented as a live-action Punch and Judy show.

Character: Fudgie
Age: 30s-40s
Genre: Comedic

Scene Synopsis: Fatboy's wife, Fudgie, is greedy, just like her husband. She plans to rent out a room in their house to make extra money and get extra attention without Fatboy knowing.

Notes:

THEMES: GREED, MARRIAGE, SECRECY

Fatboy

FUDGIE. *(swooning)* I love that ugly sack of shit and yet I think of murder. Just stab him in the head forty or fifty times and watch him drop away dead. Beat him with a baseball bat until my arm gets tired. Suffocate him in his fitful sleep. I have myself to think of, after all. I was not born, brought screaming into this world, delivered like a package, to be poor. My parents' indiscretion was not to result in this. I am of noble lineage. I have the charts. My profile belongs on coins. I'm the brains of this outfit is what I'm saying and don't you ever forget it. He can strut, he can swagger, but I'm deep below. I'm tracking it out ten moves away. Proof? I'll give you proof. *(She grabs newspaper.)* Here, in the classifieds, what is this among the desperate and depraved? "Room to let. Wrong side of town. Professionals only, please." I always could turn a phrase, that last part is poetry. I placed the ad, got him out of the house and now sit back like a queen. *(She sits regally. A knock on the door.)* My god it worked. Ten words printed in the morning paper and a professional knocks on my door. This is truly the time of modern marvels, the apex of civilization. *(a knock on the door)*

(to audience) Don't tell him about Fatboy. I live alone in dignified squalor. I'm a woman to be pitied and paid. Sit up straight and look presentable. I'll do the talking.

All the King's Women
Luigi Jannuzzi

Play Synopsis: The story of Elvis Presley told through the eyes of seventeen Women! Some Enthralled! Some Appalled, ALL OBSESSED! A fast paced series of 5 comedic plays and 3 monologues based on the Life of Elvis Presley.

Character: Saleswoman
Age: 40s-50s
Genre: Comedic

Scene Synopsis: A saleswoman recounts the story of how she persuaded eleven year-old Elvis Presley to buy his first guitar as a birthday present, instead of the rifle he has his heart set on.

Notes:

All the King's Women

SALESWOMAN. When I first saw the little boy enter this hardware store, I said to myself, "My God, there is something wrong with that child," which is a heck of a thing to say about a eleven year-old holding his Mother's hand, entering a hardware store. But that's what I felt. And I remember thinking, "I don't want anything to do with this kid, I'm going to go to the bathroom, won't be my customer." And when I came back the little boy, his mom and that odd feeling were standing right in front of me. And the little boy's Mother says to me, "It's his Eleventh birthday, we're here for a present." So I say, "Isn't that wonderful, how old are you, son?" And the boy says, "Old enough for a 22 Rifle!" I look at the mother, and the mother's going like, *(shaking head no)* giving me the universal silent Mother sign for "over my dead body." So I get down, right to the level of the boy's face and I say, "Son, instead of a 22 rifle how about if I show you...a brand new...guitar?" I place the guitar on the countertop, and the mother is saying, "Son, take this now." And the kid's saying, "No." So then I hop in with my big sales line. I use this a lot 'cause everyone wants to be a country western singer. Especially around Tupelo, Mississippi 'cause everybody wants to be like Mississippi Slim. Who's a local boy. So I say, "You know who Mississippi Slim is, don't you?" The boy says, "Yes, Ma'am." And I said, "Well, you take this and learn how to play it, you may be famous someday like Mississippi Slim." And it was just at that point that I could just see the defeat in this boy's face. And I just knew this guitar ain't going nowhere but a closet. But I pushed it, I said, "Son, what is your name?" "Elvis," the kid says. And I said, "Elvis, what's your last name?" "Presley," he adds. "Elvis Presley, I'm going to remember that name," I said,"'Cause someday I might hear about you and I'm going say that I was the lady who sold him his first guitar when he wanted a rifle." Of course, the kid's having nothing of the humor here. And the mother's nodding, "That's right you may be another Mississippi Slim, Elvis." I took the twelve dollars, ninety-five cents. I reached over the counter, gave him a bag of pics, a tuning pipe, a handful of lollipops. Said, "Happy eleventh birthday!" The little boy said, "Thank you, Ma'am." Walked out.

THEMES: FAMILY, MEMORY, PERSUASION

Gorgons
from Gorgons and Other Plays

Don Nigro

Play Synopsis: When Ruth, an aging star, secures the role of a lifetime in a film called *The Gorgons,* she desperately needs a co-star to gain funding. Convinced that Mildred, her life-long rival, is the one up for the task, Ruth gives a grand performance to persuade her. But once on set of the horror film, their rivalry grows a bit more dangerous than either anticipated.

Character: Ruth
Age: 40s-60s
Genre: Comedic

Scene Synopsis: Ruth corners Mildred in Mildred's dressing room after a performance. After failing to charm Mildred with false flattery, Ruth cuts to the chase about why she's come to see Mildred.

Notes:

Gorgons

RUTH. Listen, sweetheart. Just clamber down off your high horse
for a minute, get out your ear trumpet and try to pay attention
before the arteries in your brain harden. It wasn't easy for me
to come here tonight, you know. This place is as cold as a meat
locker and it smells like putrefying raccoons. The seats are so
hard I've got permanent nerve damage in my buttocks, and
I'd rather watch cheese mold grow than sit through one more
of these dismal old flatulent jabberfests that pass for legitimate
drama, but it just so happens there's a wonderful role for me
in this film, the meatiest part I've been offered in years, and
it simply won't work unless I have somebody of almost but
not quite equal stature playing opposite me so the force of
my incredibly powerful presence won't blast her right off the
screen. I know I'm not your favorite person in the world, and
Lord knows, you're not the prom date of my dreams, either,
but believe it or not this is actually a halfway decent script.
At least the two female leads are not entirely insipid. They're
both really very strong. And it's not Lesbians. It's sisters. Just
read it, will you? If you don't like it, I'll get Gloria Swanson. I
know she'd give her remaining four teeth to do it.

THEMES: AMBITION, RIVALRY, PERSUASION

Showtime at First Baptist

Ron Osborne

Play Synopsis: To raise spirits and funds for the rebuilding of the First Baptist of Ivy Gap church, the women of the congregation plan an evening of entertainment designed to showcase the congregation's talent. Under the direction of Edith, the pastor's wife, the ladies devise a song and dance number that may shock the congregation. Change is in the air as these six diverse women challenge institutions as well as each other.

Character: Olene
Age: 50s
Genre: Comedic

Scene Synopsis: Fed up with the old-fashioned customs of her sleepy Southern church, Olene vows to bring progress from the outside world to Ivy Gap.

Notes:

Showtime at First Baptist

OLENE. Why is everybody staring at me? All day! Everybody
staring. Like I'm a creature from another planet. Y'all need
to know something this is what women outside of Podunk,
Tennessee wear these days! *(modeling her outfit and proud of it)*
Bright, festive colors fashionable style fabric that clings *(now
whirling to show off the cling, seductively)* shows there's a differ-
ence in the sexes. If all those those *(Points to the sanctuary. Not
knowing the right disparaging word.)* Baptists. If they only knew
the things going on other places – Diseases have been cured,
man has walked on the moon women have gone from nylons
to panty hose to nothing – Yet here, the Middle Ages still rule!
As God is my witness, Mae Ellen, I'll bring this church! Ivy
Gap! into the 1970s! Kicking and screaming if I have to! Just
you watch!

DRAMATIC MONOLOGUES

MALE

Fall

Bridget Carpenter

Play Synopsis: Lydia's parents are making her go with them to family swing camp, and she's less than thrilled. However, her self-imposed isolation gives way when Mr. Gonzales, her mother's quiet colleague, begins to pay attention to her. She learns to dance; she allows herself to fall in love. When Lydia's dance teacher Gopal reveals Lydia's secret, her family is unexpectedly tested.

Character: Mr. Gonzales
Age: 20s
Genre: Dramatic

Scene Synopsis: Mr. Gonzales tells an inquisitive, fourteen year-old Lydia about the last memory of his mother.

Notes:

Fall

MR. GONZALES. When I was five, my mother, my father and me came here to the seaside. A picnic. My mother had made little cakes and I had brought a kite which didn't fly. There was a balloon. The kind you ride in. Dollar a ride. My mother wanted to go. Not my dad. And I was too little. So she got in the basket – and he stayed on the ground, holding my hand. The sky was no color at all. We watched my mother go up, up, up. The balloon grew smaller and smaller as the wind pushed it above the low clouds. She was just a tiny...thing...in the basket. And I let go of my father's hand, I jumped up and down. I held my arms high in a V to her. I waved and waved. I wanted her to see me. And she waved back! She imitated me exactly, both arms high. And then she was in the air. Arms still waving. I watched her fall. She was dark against the pale sky, a doll. When I looked up at my father, his hair had turned white. And instead of running in the direction where she fell, he turned his back. He never spoke my mother's name aloud again. He could not forgive her for leaning out too far. He could not forgive me for... And – why should he. Why should he.

THEMES: FAMILY, DEATH, GUILT

That Pretty Pretty; or, The Rape Play
Sheila Callaghan

Play Synopsis: A pair of radical feminist ex-strippers scour the country on a murderous rampage against right-wing pro-lifers, blogging about their exploits. Meanwhile, a scruffy screenwriter named Owen tries to bang out his magnum opus in a hotel room. When Owen decides to incorporate the strippers into his screenplay, the boundaries of reality begin to blur, and only a visit from Jane Fonda can help keep worlds from blowing apart.

Character: Owen
Age: 20s
Genre: Dramatic

Scene Synopsis: Owen's fantasy is taking over as he begins to put himself into different characters while working on his novel.

Notes:

That Pretty Pretty; or, The Rape Play

OWEN. Thank you, Jane…

(OWEN steps into the gown.)

Come on, Owen. Get into it. SLUT SUPREME.

(He opens a makeup bag and begins applying makeup, facing forward.)

I am so fucking pretty. I am so fucking fucking pretty, yo. Suckas. You wanna suck lemons from my cheeks. I got fuckin' mad pretty on my shit. My pretty is like PROFOUND. It has emissions. Waves of pretty. I'm like a gas burner of pretty. Stick a pot on me I'll make it whistle. Step the fuck off, right, 'cause my pretty will eat your soul. My pretty is a black hole. I am so pretty I drain all the ugly off you and wear it like a swimsuit. GODDAMN AM I PRETTY. Holy fucking shit. You can't stand it. You are like, she is so pretty I need to BASH her. I need to tear her pubes out. I need to hate on her. That pretty is cancerous. That pretty is a little iced cookie and I need to bite it. That pretty is TOXIC. That pretty boils in my gut, it eats me up, that pretty comes to me at night and scrapes all my tender spots. Soils my boxer briefs. That pretty is FUCKED-UP, I need to poke through it with my thumbs, I need to fuck the joy out of that pretty. I want to kill that pretty. I want to kill that pretty. I want to kill that pretty.

That's what they say about me.

Masked

Ilan Hatsor, translated by Michael Taub

Play Synopsis: An explosive Israeli play about three Palestinian brothers. Set during the Intifada with the Israeli-Arab struggle as its backdrop, *Masked* depicts the tragedy of one family torn between duty, kinship, principles and survival.

Character: Na'im
Age: 20s
Genre: Dramatic

Scene Synopsis: Na'im, an eager participant of the resistance in Israel, has learned that his oldest brother, Daoud, is a traitor.

Notes:

Masked

NA'IM. What do you want from him? He has nothing to say. Every
   word he utters only buries him deeper. Just look, see what he
   tied me up with? *(waving his plastic handcuffs)* You know what
   these are, Khalid? Plastic handcuffs, from the Israeli army...
   (pause) You know, Khalid, when the Israelis first came to our
   village, I was seven...Ataf and me, we took a few other kids and
   organized an army...kids. Daoud didn't want to take part. He
   sat on a hill with the soldiers. They gave him candy, he sang and
   danced for them. I was so ashamed. Me...since I was a kid, I
   never stopped dreaming the occupation would end. *(to DAOUD)*
   And you...my brother...what do you dream of? A house? In
   Israel? You're finished.

   There's nothing for you. I heard your offer to Khalid...They'll
   stick you with hookers and junkies, on the smelliest street in
   the lousiest slum. Fifty years you'll be licking their asses, but
   you'll still be an Arab snitch who sold his people for money.
   Even Arabs in Israel will spit at you. Is that how your son will
   grow up? *(shows his tied-up hands)* Like this? In disgrace? You
   don't have to fight. If only you took it seriously...a little...in
   your heart...but no, it's all words for you. You can't turn it into
   money, it doesn't mean anything to you. Look at me. Me...I
   fight. Hard. And brutal, because I think we could make it.
   Nobody's giving away anything for free. It's a struggle! Oth-
   erwise we don't deserve what we get. What you call 'fancy
   phrases'...You, no matter how you try to turn it around, you
   sold yourself to be a slave. Nothing more. I'm not telling you
   all this just to preach. *(NA'IM, still handcuffed, embraces DAOUD.)*
   You're my big brother. I'm leaving you now. You're going to
   climb to the top of the mosque and shout into the loudspeak-
   ers for the whole village to hear. "I'm Daoud. I handed over
   your sons, I blew up your homes. I'm a squealer, this is my
   punishment. " And then you'll jump. You'll jump. It'll be fast
   and painless, and more important, it's the only way you'll save
   your name. And ours. The only way. Don't let anyone touch
   you, because if they do, you'll not only die like a dog, but your
   son will be cursed as well. Get up, my brother. Get up and
   do it.

THEMES: FAMILY, LEGACY, BETRAYAL

Terre Haute
Edmund White

Play Synopsis: A famous author comes face-to-face with America's most notorious terrorist. One has a story to write, the other has a story to tell. As the clock ticks on death row, a strange bond grows between the two men. Filled with clever sparring and raw emotion, this is a taut drama that touches on the definitions of freedom and the need for love.

Character: Harrison
Age: 20s-30s
Genre: Dramatic

Scene Synopsis: Harrison, a death row inmate, explains to a reporter how his military failure helped lead down a path of destruction.

Notes:

THEMES: Failure, Pride, Guilt

Terre Haute

HARRISON. The Gulf War was pretty big. I had always been a crack soldier but after the war I tried to get into the Green Berets but I fucked up. So when I went to Fort Bragg, North Carolina – I was feeling great. On the plane going there I was with a buddy and the pilot announced that there were two heroes of the war on board and everyone applauded – that was a very popular war, don't forget. So when I got to Fort Bragg I thought here I am, we just won a war, of course I'll get into the Special Forces but I didn't. It's a twenty-four day program – you have to swim fifty yards fully dressed with your boots on and battle uniform. You have to march 150 miles with a fifty-pound rucksack on your back. Fifty-two pushups in two minutes. I could do the pushups and the swim, though that took it out of me, the swim. I ran two miles, but it was my slowest time in two years. I had these fuckin' new boots like a moron and my feet got so bad I had to quit. Just two days in and I had to quit. And then I had to go back to my unit, defeated. I wasn't even twentythree yet. The fuckin' war had fucked me up.

THEMES: FAILURE, PRIDE, GUILT

Living Room in Africa
Bathsheba Doran

Play Synopsis: Childhood friends, Edward and Marie, have moved to a village in Africa while Edward is setting up a museum there with money from the West. Within weeks it becomes apparent that they have moved to an area devastated by AIDS. Questions about their own personal and political responsibilities become impossible to ignore.

Character: Anthony
Age: 20s-30s
Genre: Dramatic

Scene Synopsis: With the outbreak of AIDS in his village, Anthony urges Edward to move the location of his gallery outside of Africa, and take him along.

Notes:

Living Room in Africa

ANTHONY. You, you live in this big house. You don't understand how it is for me. How it is for everyone. Where I live you do not know, Edward, what I come from every day when I come to the gallery. Everyone where I live is dying! There is silence everywhere while people wait for their death to come for them. No one speaks about it, we just walk through it, we are stepping over bodies to walk to the road. No one is clearing the bodies, Edward. There are people lying outside their house, you don't know if they sleep or if they are dead now. There is a smell and there is nowhere in the village you can go that does not have that smell. Some people think you can catch it just from the smell. I think that too, sometimes, at night. But I do not understand why I think that because the smell is sweet. Step off the road and walk down the hill and you would see Africa. There are hundreds of families. With no running water, no proper doors, or windows, or beds, Edward, or chairs like these! It is nothing! Nothing! You would refuse to live this way. I refuse it too, Edward. We must build a gallery somewhere else, where people are alive and they can come to see your pictures. You know the other friends of mine who are working with us? Nick? Steve? They have a foam in their mouths. When they are talking you can see the white. They will not come back to work, after the rains. Everyone is sick! Everyone I know is sick! There is no one to work! But I can still work. We should work somewhere else. You can! You said you can! You said you know many people. You promise me, you promise me, you promise me these things. I cannot make you keep your promises.

Gee's Bend

Elyzabeth Gregory Wilder

Play Synopsis: *Gee's Bend* depicts the turbulent history of African-Americans in the 20th century by focusing on a single family in the real community of Gee's Bend, Alabama, which is now famous for the beautiful quilts created by the women that grew up there.

Character: Macon
Age: 20s-30s
Genre: Dramatic

Scene Synopsis: Macon tells Sadie a memory from his childhood that has driven him to make a better life for his family.

Notes:

Gee's Bend

MACON. I get this land so I got something to show for all the work
I do. I get this land, so my wife and my children always got a
home. When we was little, we out in the fields, working somebody else's land. I be just a little thing when I see old Van de
Graff's son come riding through here on his horse. Naked as
the Lord made him. That man was crazy. He go up and down
the rows of cotton tossing pennies into the dirt. Yelling to the
mens, "Here chickie, chickie, chickie." And them mens come
crowding around, pushing at one another hoping they find
a penny or two that man done thrown down. I see my daddy
down on his knees and I say to myself, "Won't never see me
like that." Van de Graff sees me just standing there and yells
out, "Pick up them pennies, boy." But I don't move. Everybody
stops. Looks. "Pick 'em up." He starts throwing them pennies,
one at a time. Hitting me in the head. But I stand there, stone
still. 'til that man come round on that horse and kicks me to
the ground. We get home that night and my daddy just about
beat me dead. Tells me I made a fool a him. Like I ain't been
taught better. He beat me cause he want me to learn.

But I make my own promise that day. I promise myself I
won't take no hand out from no body. You be the one on the
ground, the only place you got to look is up. So that's what I
do. I say to myself, You keep looking up, one day you be there.
And here I am. With a new house and a new wife and a new
baby coming up.

THEMES: FAMILY, DETERMINATION, HOPE

Water & Power

Richard Montoya

Play Synopsis: *Water & Power* is modern noir. What emerges from the long shadows of a rainy night is as mysterious as what will never see the light of day. Who is the Power behind the Power? How does Water flow in a desert? Who controls the streets, cops, gangs or gangsters in suits and ties? Nothing is concrete in L.A. except the river.

Character: Power
Age: 20s-30s
Genre: Dramatic

Scene Synopsis: At 4am, in a dive motel room, Power tells his brother how grief has shaped him, how all that he has seen on the drive pushed him, and how the sound of bagpipes haunts him.

Notes:

Water & Power

POWER. Bagpipes. I want bagpipes. You be sure I have them. We play them across the street when we bury cops. I've lost a lot of brothers already. The politicians change, you guys come and go, but the bagpipes remain. *(Power points toward the cathedral.)* There. *(pointing to his head)* Here. Bagpipes. Damn, I hate the feeling of power they give me. So real you know? Rows and rows of cops, sheriffs from all over the country. Standing at attention in the cathedral courtyard for hours in the hot sun. Nobody moving out of reverence for a fallen brother. Patrol cars lined up from here to Chinatown. Engine ladders crossed, the flag hanging over Temple and Grand Avenue. Carefully fold the flag that was draped over the coffin, pass it to the widow. She is weary of our remembrance faces. Sometimes the child of a Fallen Officer is so young they think every cop is their father. What do you say to that, bro? What do you tell that child? So I ask my God Cop in my best white voice: what do you want from me? And I make my little deals with him. He wants me to take my grief and turn it into power. That power is the bullets coming out of my sidearm. It's the baton crashing down on the next cleanly shaven head. My God is righteous, bro. And righteous are the Peacekeepers. I am a monster, but he forgives me because I am a monster built of dead cops and bagpipes. They built this Dark House. One cop funeral at a time.

THEMES: DEATH, POWER, GRIEF

Cell

Judy Klass

Play Synopsis: *Cell* is a murder mystery – to about the same extent that Sophocles' *Oedipus Rex* is a murder mystery. Lieutenant Rodriguez questions Dennis Kadman about his older brother Michael, who has OD'd on heroin in Dennis' apartment. All Dennis wants to know is: who gave Michael the drugs?

Character: Dennis
Age: 20s-30s
Genre: Dramatic

Scene Synopsis: When Dennis finds out that he gave his brother, Michael, the lethal dose of morphine, Dennis reacts to his brother's calculated plan.

Notes:

Cell

DENNIS. You didn't want anyone else to do it. This was the play you wanted to write. It's good to see you finally complete a project, Michael. A lot of forethought and planning and stick-with-it-ness went into this. It makes me proud. I came in and saw you with the foam on your lips. And tried to tell myself that you were sleeping. But I knew. I knew right away. It's not you anymore. Just an ugly old house, with nobody home. A fat bag of bones. They can burn it, bury it, I don't care what they do with it. You're gone, your mind, your mind. And I'm more alone than I was during all the years you were gone. I'm all alone, for real. You know, when I moved you in, I kind of wanted to move my bed out here, to be across the room from yours. Like when we were little, and I was in my crib, and then my cot, and you were across the room, on your bed. And you'd read to me, and talk with me, and then after Mom shut out the light, you'd whisper to me, and recite. And I used to drift off to the sound of your voice. I think I was the happiest baby in the whole world. And when you were a shit to me later, when you wouldn't talk, when you'd play those mind-fucking games, I'd still remember that. Being a baby, and drifting off to that voice. I'd think: this is not my brother. This is an impostor damaged by drugs. But then sometimes, my brother would peep through at me. And then I'd realize: that was one of the mind-fuck games. You'd say: "I'll hold the ball, Charlie Brown, and you come running up and kick it!" Like Lucy. And I'd fall for it. I'd go flying, and land on my ass, every time. And then when you'd disappear, and Mom would be staggering around the house, hysterical – I could never touch anything in the room. It was never really my room, always yours. I couldn't sleep in your bed. They wouldn't have wanted that. All through high school, when you were long gone, I just wandered in the ruins of your world. I'd pick up notebooks, old DC comic books off the shelf, looking for clues. Peanuts books. And I'd try to complete the process you'd started, of shaping me. I threw myself into causes and ideas you'd discarded long ago. I wanted to be good enough, I wanted to understand enough so that you'd come back and be proud of me. Fuck you for walking out on me, again and again and again. Fuck you for snatching that football away. I wanted to kill you so many times. I never would have done it. I never would have hurt you. Fuck you for tricking me into doing it.

THEMES: BETRAYAL, LOSS, FAMILY

The Thread Men
from Off Off Broadway Festival Plays, 33rd Series

Thomas C. Dunn

Play Synopsis: John, a self-important psychiatrist, is trapped in an elevator with Addelin, a sinister stranger with a chip on his shoulder. But as John begins to lose patience with Addelin, he quickly learns that his decisions both past and present may have life or death consequences.

Character: Addelin
Age: 20s-30s
Genre: Dramatic

Scene Synopsis: Addelin describes his father's drawn-out, unfortunate death to John who is quickly losing his patience with the situation.

The Thread Men

ADDELIN. *(laughing)* Is that a professional opinion? You want to know dark, John? Let me explain it to you. As a little kid I grew up with my grandparents and around five, six years old, my grandfather got sick. The doctor said bronchitis. My grandmother gave him some medicine but he still had this...hacking cough. That's not even it. This cough was like...the scraping of your insides. My grandfather would just lay in bed screaming between coughs that there was some goddamn hair spray in his throat. He was convinced that someone in the house was filling his room with hair spray every time he fell asleep. Well, for the first week, you know, my grandmother, my two aunts who lived with us, they wouldn't go near hair spray or any kind of spray, out of concern. But two weeks later my grandfather's still coughing and coughing and telling them he can't even breathe. But what are they going to do, right? Not use spray bottles to clean the house? Let their hair go to shit? So a little spray here and there. Within two weeks, they're spraying it on thick, telling him to shut up, that it's all in his mind. So that's it. All that pain is in his mind. His whole lower face is covered with phlegm and drool because he's tired of wiping it off. His body's slick with sweat and his stomach is distorted. You know the muscles, from contracting and contracting, night and day...they're just bulging out of this emaciated body. And he's screaming fucking bloody murder, 'the hair spray, the hair spray.' But the pain's in his mind, so they just ignore him. When I found him the doctor said he'd been dead for two days, suffocated on some combination of phlegm and vomit. It was probably the paint on the walls or... they denied him his suffering and dignity in death because they couldn't understand the pain. They couldn't see it, they couldn't feel it, so they just convinced themselves it shouldn't be there at all.

THEMES: DEATH, PAIN, FAMILY

My First Time

Ken Davenport

Play Synopsis: *My First Time* features four actors in hysterical and heartbreaking stories about first sexual experiences written by real people. Their stories are silly, sweet, absurd, funny, heterosexual, homosexual, shy, sexy, and everything in between.

Character: Man #2
Age: 20s-40s
Genre: Dramatic

Scene Synopsis: A young man recounts his first sexual encounter to the audience.

Notes:

My First Time

MAN #2. I didn't learn the woman's name. I didn't even get a good look at her face. I had a fight with my girlfriend. In an effort to cheer me up, my father, Karl, took me to his annual convention. I didn't see any wives there and the entertainment reflected it. There were some business meetings but we didn't attend. The last night I begged off claiming a headache. I was in a sound sleep when a naked woman climbed into bed with me. I was aroused before I fully came to. She threw a leg over me and inserted me. I thought I was in a wet dream initially. The cigarettes on her breath...I did what I was supposed to do mostly to get it over with. I wish I had thrown her out but I didn't. The pain was compounded by Karl having a woman of his own in the other bed. I noticed a condom on the floor beside Karl's bed but my woman didn't use one. Karl's answer was that my woman didn't need one since this was my first time. He was never "Dad" after that, but "Karl." I have since forgiven myself, as there is only so much you can ask of a fifteen year-old boy.

THEMES: FAMILY, SEX, FORGIVENESS

The Kind that Doesn't Budge
from Truth be Told

Lisa Soland

Play Synopsis: *Truth Be Told* is a full-length play that consists of eleven, one-person stories shared by a variety of personalities, all focused on getting at the truth.

Character: Todd
Age: 20s-40s
Genre: Dramatic

Scene Synopsis: Answering a friend who has just asked if he's afraid of commitment, Todd reminsices longingly about the kind of "love that doesn't budge" that he felt towards his second grade teacher.

Notes:

The Kind that Doesn't Budge

TODD. No, no. It's not the commitment thing. It's just well… *(hesitant)* When I was in second grade, I had this teacher – Mrs. Moore. I didn't have a crush on her or anything. It wasn't like that. She was just…amazing. *(beat)* She was plain but smart. Man, she never forgot a thing. And we all wanted to please her for some reason. Just make her happy somehow. *(beat)* She had this long, black hair. Beautiful, shiny, sort of bluish, you know? – when the light hit it just right. And she always wore it up, in a tight bun. Always. Every day. This perfect, round bun, neatly gathered above her neck. *(beat)* Mrs. Moore had a son, Danny. He was my buddy and we would go to each other's houses a lot, you know – hang out. *(beat)* One time I was over there and we were getting ready for bed, brushing our teeth and I walk down the hall to the bathroom and pass by his mother's room. The door was open. It was just a quick look, you know – a glance, but I saw her sitting at this table with a mirror in front of her and she had her hair, her beautiful hair down, brushing it with one of those, you know, those old fashioned brushes with the ivory handles. She was wearing a robe, a blue robe and her hair fell all the way down to her waist. *(thinking back)* Brushing. Just brushing. *(pause)* I was speechless. Couldn't talk for days. *(beat)*

Well, a couple of months ago I went back for my high school reunion and got together with Danny. He was back living with his mother in that same house. His mom, my second grade teacher had Alzheimer's. Has Alzheimer's. *(beat)*

She didn't remember me. I guess something inside of me hoped she would. But she didn't. And her long, black hair was still long but gray – kinky, worn, and pulled into some sort of tangled mess in the back. It looked like it hadn't been brushed in weeks. I sat there at the kitchen table and watched them, the two of them, fight down her lunch. She wouldn't eat. But Danny sat there. He sat there getting food spit all over him and he didn't budge. He didn't budge. *(beat)* It's not that I want a woman like that, with long hair or anything. I just remember that kind of…commitment. That kind of love. The kind that doesn't budge. That's what I want. That's what I'm waiting for.

THEMES: COMMITMENT, LOVE, LONGING

Quint and Miss Jessel at Bly

Don Nigro

Play Synopsis: Peter Quint is sent by his lifelong employer, the Master of Bly, to be the servant in charge of a remote English country house where Miss Jessel has just arrived to be governess to the orphaned children of the master's brother. The ultimately deadly love triangle that results forms a darkly funny and erotic Gothic love story.

Character: Quint
Age: 30s
Genre: Dramatic

Scene Synopsis: Quint casts his spell over the reserved Miss Jessel by sharing the macabre, exotic dreams that haunt the children, Miles and Flora. He then ventures to share suggestive dreams he's had, many times the subject being Miss Jessel herself.

Notes:

THEMES: SECRECY, DESIRE, LONGING

Quint and Miss Jessel at Bly

QUINT. I wouldn't bring it up at all, were it not for the fact that the children are also having bad dreams. They've told me about them. Don't they tell you their dreams? I thought they might. I know they're reasonably fond of you. They've told me so. And I have no particular cause to suspect they would lie to me about a thing like that. They are, generally speaking, as far as I can tell, relatively truthful children, most of the time, and I think I can say without hesitation that the children are genuinely fond of you. I have absolute confidence in saying that. *(pause)* India. The children have dreams about India. The Punjab. The Ganges. Bombay and Nagpur. Mosquito nets draped over the corpses of dead Europeans. The rivers are brown and full of dead oxen. Snakes in the reeds. Crumbling temples. Elephants. Water buffalo. Camels mating. Crocodiles waddling lightning quick up the river bank to snatch unsuspecting infants in their jaws. Barefoot, haunted people in the narrow streets of Poona. Gorgeous dark-eyed women with somewhat annoying accents. A cacophany of Bengali, Hindustani, and Urdu. In the children's dreams, their parents are dying, their faces pasty and rotting. At night they come to look in the windows, trickles of blood running out the corners of their mouths. In their dreams the children wander the corridors of labyrinthine temples while snakes crawl up carvings of seven-breasted, twelve-armed dancing goddesses, and their parents lie naked in their beds, sweating from tropical fever, and hallucinating about Wembley. *(pause)* Whereas I, on the other hand, merely dream about you. Except now and then I also dream that somebody is looking in the windows. Outside looking in. And then, in my dream, I see that the face of that person is my face. I am the one who is outside looking in the windows, in my dream. And do you know what I see, Miss Jessel, when I'm looking in the windows, in my dream? Two naked figures, straining together in the darkness.

In the Sawtooths

Dano Madden

Play Synopsis: Oby, Nellie, and Darin have been friends since high school. Now in their thirties, they have become busier in their lives, but one thing remains constant: their annual backpacking adventure. As their trip nears, their lives are suddenly shattered by tragedy. What ensues is a true test of an old friendship. Can they remain friends as they desperately try to navigate through an immense and unexpected wilderness?

Character: Darin
Age: 30s
Genre: Dramatic

Scene Synopsis: Nellie, Oby, and Darin, competitive as they are, enjoy sharing stories while out on their camping trips. Here Darin tells the story of a hike he was on as a boy, which for obvious reasons stands out in his memory.

Notes:

In the Sawtooths

DARIN. I began hiking as a boy with my father. He taught me everything I know about hiking and safety. So my dad and I went on a trip one year up to the panhandle, right along the Montana border – grizzly bear country. Out on the trail, just the two of us, amazing view, I start to fall behind. My dad always hikes really fast and he thought, he thought I should keep up. But I lose sight of him. There's a huge bend in the trail and just as I turn the corner I see two bear cubs – romping in the grass. I freeze. Watching them. My dad taught me never to approach animals – even babies. I'm actually having a really fun time, watching them run around and tackle each other. I'm watching, I'm watching and suddenly I get a real uneasy feeling. Like I'm being watched. And I turn around, real slowly, and right behind me is a grizzly. No growling. Just staring. I can't move. She inches closer, her nose is right in my face. I can feel her breath. And, I start to cry. Quietly. The mama stares a little longer. And finally, she just goes around me, back to her cubs and they disappear into the valley. *(pause)* My dad still feels guilty about that.

THEMES: FAMILY, DISCOVERY, FEAR

The Four of Us

Itamar Moses

Play Synopsis: What if all your dreams came true...for your best friend? *The Four of Us* follows Ben, whose first novel vaults him into literary stardom, and his friend David, a struggling playwright, who is thrilled by Ben's success...and crushed by it. From the dreams of aspiring youth to the realities of adulthood, this poignant two-man comedy explores friendship and memory, the gap between our hopes and our lives, and the struggles between our egos and our capacity to love.

Character: David
Age: 30s
Genre: Dramatic

Scene Synopsis: David reveals an upsetting revelation about his relationship to his best friend.

Notes:

The Four of Us

DAVID. Okay. We're lying in bed together, you know…after…and
we're going to sleep, and I just have this thought, this one,
stray, like, rogue, thought, just creeps in, just sort of flits across
my brain, and the thought is: what if I feel absolutely nothing for this person. That was it. That was the thought. What
if I feel nothing. And suddenly. I mean. It was like my heart…
stopped. Or like I fell through ice. Or like. If my life was a
movie? Like I was the hero, and I had won, I got the girl, and
the credits rolled, and, but, instead of it being over, and me
being allowed to get up and, you know, leave, instead I was
still stuck in the movie, and, even worse, everybody around me
still believed the movie was real, and was still in character, and
I had to, like, play along, but with no actual sentiment behind
it, I mean, seriously, I just wanted to turn to her right there, in
the dark, and say, "Hey. Remember when I said I loved you?
What a great scene that was. Okay! That's a wrap! Maybe we'll
work together again someday!" Only I can't do that. I mean:
obviously. I mean: I don't want to want to. Because until like
a second before that, literally, like a second before, everything
felt so good. Just…fine. And then I have this one thought and
everything just, like, inverted, like a photo negative, or… And
not just with this girl but suddenly I started seeing everything
this way. From that moment. I, literally, I have been literally
dividing my life, you know, mentally, into the moment before
I had that thought, and the moment after I had that thought.
This one…thought. And I – What I want is to go back to how it
was. To feel how I felt a while ago about her and about everything I want to…undo…whatever has taken place, and not
ever ever ever feel this way again.

Neighborhood 3: Requisition of Doom
Jennifer Haley

Play Synopsis: In an upscale subdivision with identical houses, parents find their teenagers addicted to an online horror video game. The game setting? A subdivision with identical houses. The goal? Smash through an army of zombies to escape the neighborhood for good. But as the line blurs between virtual and reality, both parents and players realize that fear has a life of its own.

Character: Steve
Age: 30s-40s
Genre: Comedic

Scene Synopsis: Steve can't find his daughter, Chelsea, and fears her disappearance is linked to her video game addiction.

Notes:

Neighborhood 3: Requisition of Doom

STEVE. my only daughter
chelsea
is hooked on one
Neighborhood
something
i don't know
but when i say
hooked
i guess i'm
putting it mildly
she basically plays this
every waking moment
from the time she gets
  home from school
to the time she goes to bed
if she goes to bed
we bought her a
high speed gaming com-
  puter
for christmas
we thought that would make
  her
happy
we didn't know
we'd never see her again
she gets online
and plays this character
with other people online
playing characters
some of them
are her friends
but some of them
for all i know
could be pedophiles
they conspire for hours
on that instant message
and conference calls
they run around a Neigh-
  borhood

that looks very much like
ours
butchering Zombies
who look a whole lot like
us
but let's see
what am i worried about
i'm worried that
she's not making real friends
  in the
real world
the way she looks
no one at school will
talk to her
when i was a kid
i made bombs out of fire-
  crackers
and my folks thought i was
possessed
and of course they were
overreacting
and
i've threatened to
remove the computer
but i don't know if it is the
  computer
or if it's
i'm a
corporate manager
i manage people at all levels
and when they're not up to
  task i just
fire them
but you know
you can't fire your only kid
even when she comes out of
  her room
looking like some kind of
monster.

THEMES: FAMILY, FEAR, ADOLESCENCE

Sixty Miles to Silver Lake
Dan LeFranc

Play Synopsis: A moving car. A father and son. The father drives. The son's face is pressed against the rolled up window. A lifetime can pass in the sixty miles between a boy's soccer practice and his father's new apartment.

Character: Ky
Age: 30s-40s
Genre: Comedic

Scene Synopsis: On the car ride to his house, Ky tries to pump his teenage son for information on his ex-wife's personal life. His son, however, is unwilling to take sides.

Notes:

Sixty Miles to Silver Lake

KY. You think I like punishing you?

Believe me I wish I didn't Have To

but someone's got to teach you some Discipline

cuz you're clearly not learning any At Home

The woman's too busy Trolling the Orange County singles

scene to raise her Son properly

(small pause)

you know

there was a time when I wanted to hold those Hands for the Rest of my Life

(Ky shakes his head.)

When's the last time she cooked for you, Huh?

no Lemme guess

She doesn't have Time to provide you a Home-cooked Meal anymore

These days

She just drops some In-N-Out in front of you

shoves some Condoms into her Purse

and runs out the Door in her Fuck-Me Boots

am I right?

Now don't get me wrong

I mean your Mother's a Beautiful Woman

an Amazing Woman

but a Man can only take so much Anger and Sloth

you know?

(Ky drives.)

She manage to find a Job yet?

Is that a Yes or a No? well if she thinks I'm paying for your college on top of everything else

she's Out of Her Mind

She ever tell you about all the Blow she did in the Eighties?

Oh Yeah

A real Winner your Mom

She was Coked Up on our Wedding Day for Christ's Sake

She'd complain if we spent a little money going out to Eat twice a month

but the next thing you know she's bent over the Coffee Table with a Straw up her nose Snorting that stuff like it Grows on Trees

(Ky drives.)

You know if she's dating Anyone?

(Ky drives.)

Women

I'm telling ya

Men should know better

but They Suck our Dicks once in a while and we let em Get Away with Murder

am I right?

I guess you're uh still a little Too Young Huh?

THEMES: FAMILY, LOVE, ANGER

The Trials and Tribulations of a
Trailer Trash Housewife
Del Shores

Play Synopsis: Willi is the trailer trash housewife of the title, not necessarily of her own volition. Her abusive husband, J.D., won't let her get a job, one of her children is dead, and the other is verboten by her husband because he's gay. Her best and only friend, a large black woman who lives next door, worries about her constantly, always concerned that Willi's husband will end up killing her. But when Willi discovers her husband is cheating on her, the tables turn, and all of their lives will be affected forever.

Character: J.D.
Age: 30s-40s
Genre: Dramatic

Scene Synopsis: J.D. berates his wife for her wanting him to be at home rather than out at a bar after work.

Notes:

The Trials and Tribulations of a
Trailer Trash Housewife

J.D. Say you're sorry. Say you're sorry for trying to take away my one true pleasure in life. Say you're sorry, Willadean, for trying to take your hardworkin' husband's one true pleasure away. Say it! You sorry ungrateful ingrate. *(He starts pacing.)* You think I like haulin' asphalt from Mesquite to Tyler and back again, then to Denton and back again, then to Plano and back again, then to McKinney and back again, then to Arlington and back again? You think I like my shitty-ass job, Willadean? Look at me when I'm talkin' to you, woman! The only thing I have to look forward to ever' day is gettin' off work and havin' a couple of beers at the Spotlight to unwind before I have to come home to you. You don't understand stress woman. That's your problem. You don't know what it's like to live with failed dreams ever' day of your life. If you hadn't got pregnant with that little worthless no-count faggot, I coulda played for the Dallas Cowboys. I coulda been Roger fuckin' Stalback, Troy fuckin' Aikman if you hadn't got knocked up to trap me. I was all-district four years in a row! You just don't get it. Now just shut up and get your shitty tuna casserole out of the shitty oven and let's just eat another shitty meal. C'mon!

THEMES: FAILURE, RESENTMENT, ANGER

Elephant Sighs

Ed Simpson

Play Synopsis: Not long after moving to the small town of Randolphsburg, PA, uptight lawyer Joel Bixby is invited by Leo Applegate, an avuncular fast food connoisseur, to join a group of townsmen who meet in a ramshackle room at the edge of town. The more time he spends with them, the more apparent it becomes that each of them are just as lost as Joel. A group of delightful characters highlight this comedy about loss, loneliness, and the healing power of friendship.

Character: Joel
Age: 30s-40s
Genre: Dramatic

Scene Synopsis: At the play's conclusion, Joel thinks through his life and his decision to join the club with the other guys. He thinks of how easy it would be to give it all up, but does he really want to?

Notes:

Elephant Sighs

JOEL. When I was a little boy. They used to push me down. The other children, on the playground. During recess. You see, I had a stutter and the children used to make fun of the way I the way I...talked. They called me "Ja-ja-joel." And then they'd chase me. All over the playground. My whole class, maybe twenty-five boys and girls. A whole herd of kids. I'd run and run but sooner or later they'd catch me and push me down. *(beat)* And then jump on top of me. In a big pile. I was at the bottom. *(beat)* It was hard to breathe sometimes. Ever since, whenever I feel threatened I...well, that's why I... flinch...so big. Self-protection. Every morning, I wake up and for a few moments I feel somehow...disoriented. I lie in bed, eyes closed, and I'm a blank. I forget where I am. Nothing hurts. I feel...nothing. I remember nothing. And that is the only time of the day I am not afraid. I look forward to those few moments. But as soon as I realize I'm not afraid I remember who I am and what I am and I realize that I'm petrified and I remember that I am always petrified. I woke up this morning, looked at my wife, looked out my window at my backyard... and said to myself "What the hell am I doing? I can't do this anymore. I have to leave." And I started...well – musing about how easy it would be to just walk out the front door, drive to the bank, take out all our savings, gas up the car and just... hit the road. Nothing was stopping me. It was so compelling. Just the idea of leaving everything behind, starting all over again somewhere else. I even chose an alias! "Logan Douglas." I mean, Logan Douglas? That frightened me more than anything. Why would I come up with an alias unless I was serious? I love my wife. I love my family. The last thing in the world I want to do is leave. My God. But – *(A pause. Then)* What am I doing? What the hell am I doing?

Make Believe

Kristin Anna Froberg

Play Synopsis: Natasha Lisenko is twenty-two years old, clever, creative, can describe the plot of every episode of *Battlestar Galactica*, and hasn't left the house in five years. Her sister, Lena, is an energetic, popular, occasionally cruel high-school cheerleader – or was, the last time Natasha saw her. As Natasha works her way through delayed adolescence and a strangely evolving relationship with her tutor, her family works to move forward without a sister, without a daughter, and without answers to the questions surrounding her disappearance.

Character: Mike
Age: 50s
Genre: Dramatic

Scene Synopsis: Still struggling with the gruesome circumstances surrounding his daughter's death, Mike finds it difficult to control himself. When the Anderson family's sympathy card arrives, Mike finds an outlet for his grief.

Notes:

THEMES: Grief, Death, Anger

Make Believe

MIKE. Rite Aid, looks like. $2.99. Now tell me, how long do you think it took Mom's friend Mrs. Anderson to pick out this card? Keep in mind it was probably somewhere in the middle of the list, in between picking up toilet paper and dropping off film. Well, considering that the poem inside would seem to have been composed by a third grader – with a learning disability – I'm only stating it for the record, Lydia. Let's see what Natasha thinks. Sport, do you think the words "could" and "world" rhyme? Here we have a signature. Underneath the "poem." These people couldn't bring themselves to write a message – "The Anderson Family." If memory serves me correctly, Melissa and Dave have children. What are their names; I'm drawing a blank – Chelsea and Taylor. And about how old are Chelsea and Taylor these days? I think they're in high school. There's no reason they should be bothered to sign the card, there's no use for anything beyond one person scrawling "The Anderson Family" at the bottom of this – can you really call it a poem? I can't. There's no reason at all. $2.99 is perfectly sufficient. It's only our daughter's body, in the woods – I can see it right now, Lydia, Melissa Anderson's shopping list. Batteries, ink cartridge, and right in the middle, a card for the people whose daughter needed dental records to be identified. They might care, Lydia, they might care exactly two dollars and ninety-nine cents worth – plus sales tax – but they can't mean it because they can't understand unless it's their daughter in pieces in a bag. And one of these days I almost hope it is. I hope it is.

The Whipping Man

Matthew Lopez

Play Synopsis: It is April, 1865. The Civil War is over and throughout the south, slaves are being freed, soldiers are returning home and in Jewish homes, the annual celebration of Passover is being celebrated. Into the chaos of war-torn Richmond comes Caleb DeLeon, a young Confederate officer who has been severely wounded. He finds his family's home in ruins and abandoned, save for two former slaves, Simon and John, who wait in the empty house for the family's return. As the three men wait for signs of life to return to the city, they wrestle with their shared past, the bitter irony of Jewish slave-owning and the reality of the new world in which they find themselves.

Character: Simon
Age: 50s
Genre: Dramatic

Scene Synopsis: When Simon discovers that Caleb has been keeping from him that his wife and child were sold down river just before the end of the war, he is overcome with anger and grief. But he will no longer be silent.

Notes:

The Whipping Man

SIMON. You think I didn't know, Caleb, what you was doing with my daughter? I been around houses in town. I seen what happens to slave girls there. I know how it was. YOU OWNED HER! You loved her? How did you love her, Caleb? Like a dog. You love a dog, you feed a dog. But when he acts up, you also beat a dog. You might have thought you loved Sarah but you also owned her. And if this hadn't all just happened, you would have owned your baby, too. You would have owned your own child, Caleb. You don't know how it was. You don't know what this was. You don't have any idea. This is what this was. *(Simon takes off his shirt to reveal a horrible patchwork of scars on his back from various whippings through his life.)* You see this? From the Whipping Man. From your father, too. And from your grandfather. I got your family tree right here on my back. You see? Your wounds are gonna heal. You gonna rebuild your city. You gonna rejoin your nation. You gonna be a citizen. What are we gonna be? What are we gonna have? We gonna have these. You gonna go on with your life and forget you ever had a family of slaves living in your house. Forget all about us. But we always gonna remember. We gonna have the proof of it every time we look at ourselves, at our skin, on our backs. Our skin gonna remind us for the rest of our lives and our children's lives. And now your children's lives, too, Caleb. This is your legacy. This is your family's legacy.

Lions

Vince Melochi

Play Synopsis: It's the 2007 NFL season and the Detroit Lions are on a winning streak – unfortunately out of work steelworker John Waite is not. With humor and humanity, playwright Vince Melocchi offers a glimpse into The Tenth Ward Club, where the patrons place their hopes on their team, and attempt to escape the creeping demise of their city and of their way of life.

Character: Reverend Stuvants
Age: 50s
Genre: Dramatic

Scene Synopsis: Curtis complains to his friends about his grocery bagging job, but Reverend Stuvants, as the voice of reason, tries to make him see that this is one test that Curtis must face in order to fulfill the bigger picture of his life.

Notes:

THEMES: DEATH, FAITH, DETERMINATION

Lions

REVEREND STUVANTS. I am lucky. I am blessed. I found my calling when I was a boy. My father passed away from heart disease as a very young man. I was so angry at the Lord that I demanded to know why he would steal from my mother and her five children, see, I have three brothers and a sister...why he would steal from us such a righteous, honest hard-working, God-fearing man like my father. I was beside myself. Walked up to Reverend Brown, looked him in the eye and said,"I hate God. I hate you. And I want my father back." He took me in his arms, held me tight and said, "Son, I feel your pain. World ain't always right, world ain't always fair, and I ain't got the answers for you. But I can tell you this. The good Lord needed a great man to lead his people in heaven, so he called on your father for assistance. He took him because he knew...he knew you had the strength to lead your family here on earth." It was how he said it. Looked me in the eye and talked to me. Talked to me. He made me feel whole. I came back the next day, and the next. His door was always open. He taught me there is no more noble purpose in life than to help your fellow man in times of great need and despair. You need to see the big picture. The Lord has surrounded us all with love and life. How can a man measure the beauty of life without a setback or two? Adversity is just a beast reminding us how wonderful things are when it is not present. These are all tests. Tests.

THEMES: DEATH, FAITH, DETERMINATION

French Gold
from Rat Wives and Other Plays

Don Nigro

Play Synopsis: In *French Gold*, it's 1950, and David Armitage, a 70 year-old poet and former cryptographer, sits in the tangled overgrowth of his garden. The death of his housekeeper and long time friend Sarah have left him nearly alone in the huge old wreckage of the Pendragon house. An unexpected visit with his restless niece, Becky, provides an opportunity for a connection as David shares some wisdom with Becky who is on the verge of abandoning her children and running away.

Character: Davey
Age: 70s
Genre: Dramatic

Scene Synopsis: A chance moment alone with his troubled niece allows Davey to share some wisdom he's gained from life experience. He reflects on his friendship with a woman named Sarah and tries to explain the ephemeral nature of life and the futility of running away.

Notes:

French Gold

DAVEY. Cryptography. All things are written in cryptograms. Life and death are a labyrinth of cryptographic symbols, magical formulas we can no longer decipher. And my friend Sarah lies now under fresh earth. I don't know what to make of that. I never have. You know, I ran away from here, to escape this place and all its ghosts, and then I ran back here, to escape what I found when I got to wherever the hell it was I thought I went to. But this place was where I went to, and where I went to was always here in this demented garden surrounded by the labyrinth of the house where my father brooded once upon his betrayals, where generations of our kind have made love, died, and come to mourn. Something is buried here, something we can't quite get to, something very close that we just can't see. I am slowly turning into my ancestors. We always turn into the people we try to escape. You will too. But there is no other place. The wind blows leaves about in Sibyl's cave in all possible combinations, but no journey is to anyplace but back. Time moves in one direction on the surface, devouring as it goes, but inside it's always moving backwards to the past. All we can do is hold on to the people closest to us in the labyrinth, pass on whatever love is possible from each to the next, as best we can. It's buried deep inside us, the capacity to love unreasonably, hopelessly, no matter what. It's there, like lost French gold. Sarah knew. Sarah loved you.

DRAMATIC MONOLOGUES

FEMALE

Crooked

Catherine Trieschmann

Play Synopsis: Fourteen year-old Laney arrives in Oxford, Mississippi with a twisted back, a mother in crisis, and a burning desire to be writer. When she befriends Maribel Purdy, a fervent believer in the power of Jesus Christ to save her from the humiliations of high school, Laney embarks on a hilarious spiritual and sexual journey that challenges her mother's secular worldview and threatens to tear their fragile relationship apart.

Character: Maribel
Age: Teens
Genre: Dramatic

Scene Synopsis: Maribel is a passionate and well-intentioned teen who just can't help herself when it comes to talking to her new-found (non-religious) friend about Jesus.

Notes:

Crooked

MARIBEL. I get sinned against all the time in this school – Deedee
Cummings pulled down my pants in gym class today – but I
don't mind, because I know that the things of this earth,
they're not lasting. *(pause)* You think I'm a freak, don't you?
Yes, you do. I can tell. I know it's kinda freaky to bring up Jesus
when I've only just met you, but look at it this way: I mean, you
could die tomorrow, you could die this afternoon – you know
a car wreck, or a heart attack or something – and at least, I
would know that you didn't die not ever having heard of Jesus,
and maybe, just maybe, because of this conversation, because
I talked to you about Jesus, when those headlights are facing
the passenger seat and you know you're about to meet your
end, you'll remember Jesus and how much he loves you and
you'll ask him into your heart right then and there before you
die, and then you won't have to face everlasting hell.

Make Believe
Kristin Anna Froberg

Play Synopsis: Natasha Lisenko is twenty-two years old, clever, creative, can describe the plot of every episode of *Battlestar Galactica*, and hasn't left the house in five years. Her sister, Lena, is an energetic, popular, occasionally cruel high-school cheerleader – or was, the last time Natasha saw her. As Natasha works her way through delayed adolescence and a strangely evolving relationship with her tutor, her family works to move forward without a sister, without a daughter, and without answers to the questions surrounding her disappearance.

Character: Lena
Age: Teens
Genre: Dramatic

Scene Synopsis: Natasha is finally getting her act together and about to take the SAT, but Lena, in a last minute attempt to guard their sisterly bond, tries to undermine Natasha's confidence.

Notes:

Make Believe

LENA: Where are you going? Tasha. Don't go out there. TASHA. Don't go out there. Come on. Think about it. It's like a horror movie. Nobody wants you to go out there. They wouldn't. They'd be watching through their fingers. Doing the silent scream, "No, don't do it, don't do it" – 'cause everybody knows what's going to happen, the same thing that happens every time you think you like some guy, really, Tasha, you're the smart one for a reason. You'd think you'd remember. Plus, look at yourself. And so what then? Maybe you just feel so good about everything, you do so fabulous on the test. Then what? Then you go far away to some big exciting school, in some really big, exciting place, except you hate exciting places and you've never been on a plane because they crash and you're afraid and you've never actually HAD a boyfriend, Tasha, how are you going to know what do? You won't. You never know what to do. You never know what to say to people. You always say and do the exact thing you wish you hadn't, five seconds after, and then you spend hours and hours thinking about it, how are you going to be around people? How are you going to talk to people? You hate people! You needed me to make everything happen for you, and I did my best and it still wasn't enough. Even though I tried. You forget I know what the inside of your head looks like. I know what you're planning. I don't know how you think you're going to do it though. I don't know how you think you're going to do any of these big exciting things without me.

Pretty Theft

Adam Szymkowicz

Play Synopsis: After losing her father, Allegra falls under the wing of bad girl Suzy, only to find an unexpected friendship with Joe, an autistic savant. When things between them take a violent turn, Allegra and Suzy escape on a cross-country trip. The girls end up befriending Marco, a mysterious thief who claims he cannot be caught.

Character: Suzy
Age: Teens
Genre: Dramatic

Scene Synopsis: Suzy, while shoplifting, explains to her new friend why she was labeled a "slut" in school.

Notes:

Pretty Theft

SUZY. *(putting other items in her bag)* Well I wouldn't shut up, would I? When you don't shut up, the boys notice you. Course, eventually you realize no one was really listening. And you stop speaking up in class – realize maybe you weren't saying anything anyway – not something someone else couldn't say better – usually a boy. And the boys who seemed to be listening to you weren't quite the right boys. *(stuffing her pockets)* So you stopped talking. But then you realize if you lift up your shirt there are boys that like that too. But maybe those aren't quite the right boys either because then later those boys want to see what's in your pants. And want to put themselves in you even if you're not ready and maybe those aren't the right boys either but at least they need you for a few minutes. *(stuffing her bag)* Then you go after your friend's boyfriend because it's wrong and it's fun and because your friend is pretty. And you get him but once you have him, you realize he's no good. And your friend hates you. But you do it again anyway to another friend. And the girls all begin to hate you. They call you a skank and they call you a whore. But some of the boys like you some of the time. But they think you're a slut. So you embrace it because what else can you do? You buy a T-shirt that says "Fuckdoll" and a series of short skirts and you try on provocative lipsticks.

La Gringa

Carmen Rivera

Play Synopsis: María Elena García goes to visit her family in Puerto Rico during the Christmas holidays and arrives with plans to connect with her homeland. Although this is her first trip to Puerto Rico, she has had an intense love for the island – but after a while, she realizes that Puerto Rico does not welcome her with open arms. *La Gringa* is about a young woman's search for her identity.

Character: María
Age: 20s
Genre: Dramatic

Scene Synopsis: María confesses to her cousin how much her visit to Pureto Rico means to her.

Notes:

THEMES: FAMILY, BELONGING, HOME

La Gringa

MARÍA. Mami and Papi wanted me to see Europe. They felt a trip
to Europe would make me a well-rounded person...How do
you say that? Una persona más completa...I felt it was more
important to visit my country. Connect with my ancestors...
my grandmother, my great-grandmother...my family...Mami
is always talking about Puerto Rico and I wanted to see it for
myself. I have the rest of my life to see the world. I dreamt
about Puerto Rico for such a long time...El Morro was more
than I expected. I felt a true sense of history. While I was
walking around, I had this feeling of...of...peace. As my feet
touched the stones, it felt right...I was hypnotizised by the
sound of the waves crashing against the fort's walls...I realized then that I had come home...The sound of the coquis,
the smell of nature, the sun that burns your skin in one day...
Even the mosquitos bites...all are signs of welcome...I can't go
back to New York. THIS IS MY HOME. I'm staying in Puerto
Rico.

Aliens With Extraordinary Skills

Saviana Stanescu

Play Synopsis: A dark comedy about a clown from the "unhappiest country in the world," Moldova, who pins her hopes on a US work visa. Chased by Homeland Security, a deportation letter deflates Nadia's enthusiasm and a pair of spike heels might be all it takes to burst her American Dream – or turn it into a nightmare...

Character: Nadia
Age: 20s
Genre: Dramatic

Scene Synopsis: Nadia went to work a gig in place of her rommmate, Lupita. However, the "adults only" party was not what she expected. As her memory blends with the present, she describes what happened.

Notes:

Aliens With Extraordinary Skills

NADIA. Cab! Cab! *(beat)* What do you mean – "I do only Manhattan"? Washington Heights is in Manhattan! What?!...I did it... Yes...I went to a veeeery cool party. In Soho. Wall Street guys. Yes, fancy! All in expensive suits. And the women – in designer clothes, yes, like in *Sex and the City!* Perfect teeth. Perfect hair. Elegant. Stylish. Friendly. What?! I know I'm not one of them! I went there to work! To ENTERTAIN. I am a clown artist! I am somebody! What?! *(pause)* Everybody was...laughing, drinking, smoking... I learned new words in English: ganga, weed, pot, grass. Yes, drugs! They were smoking drugs, they were cool. I didn't know much about drugs. Mike noticed and laughed, he said: "She's a drug virgin." Let me explain...I get there...I am soooo excited... My heart is pumping hot steams not blood... This guy Mike ushers me in. He is confident, elegant. He says: "Hi, pretty lady." He takes my arm. He introduces me to people. He tells them: "She's from the former Soviet Union." He prepares a drink for me. A cocktail. A Cosmo! Yeah...I drink, I smoke, like everybody else...I am cool...I dance for him, for them...I am sexy, I shake it well!...A few hours pass, I think...I get tired...My stomach is a bit upset... But it doesn't matter, everything is too perfect... I walk into this room... Beautiful room... A bedroom with red-painted walls and huge windows... I can see the Hudson River...great view!... Red lights dancing on the river...like mouths with blood-red lips... I press my face on that window... My feet hurt from dancing two hours on spike heels... I take off my shoes for a moment. Just for a moment. I think I'm alone. I am not alone. Mike enters. He comes closer... I can smell his expensive aftershave... He's gonna kiss me! No. He puts his hand under my skirt...Strange... His face looks different... "Say something in Russian, Natasha!" He keeps calling me Natasha..." You, Russian babes, are all so fucking sexy"... What is he doing?... His hand...His fingers... Pushing my underwear, pushing... "C'mon, Natasha! Say FUCK ME, Mike, in Russian, Natasha!"... *(pause)* I had to run barefoot out of that room. Out of that apartment. Out and I left them there... I left my shoes... I didn't have time to grab my Manolo Blahniks... Lupita will kill me...and that's fine with me... that's fine...I deserve that. *(She sees a cab.)* Hey, cab, cab, please stop, stop, please stop! I wanna go home. Home.

THEMES: DRUGS, SEX, FEAR

Scab
Sheila Callaghan

Play Synopsis: Anima's sphere of desperation and self-destruction is invaded by the arrival of her perky new roommate, Christa. Moved by a particularly malevolent statue of the Virgin Mary and a houseplant named Susan, Anima and Christa soon enter into a profound and intimate friendship that incurs traumatic results.

Character: Anima
Age: 20s
Genre: Dramatic

Scene Synopsis: Anima recalls what she did when she found out that her father, living on the opposite side of the country, died.

Notes:

Scab

ANIMA. Boy, when I get the phone bill next month I'm going to see this date and this call and remember it was the day I lost my male parent. SO. I made phone calls up the wazoo while Mr. Helpful Caring Seaweed – sorry, he was wonderful and I am evil but I'm relatively okay with that – made a list of stuff for me and people to contact while I was gone oh fuck I have to get a plane ticket from LAX to Jersey but it will be nice to be on the east coast again because GOD I HATE IT OUT HERE no one wears black and it is always sunny and the smog gives me acne worse than a prepubescent boy working the grill at Roy Rogers and they don't even have Roy Rogers out here only Arby's can you believe that and I don't own a car and I miss the city and I miss the bars that don't close at one in the morning on a Saturday night and the rain and people who look fat and ugly in bathing suits and our creepy little Jersey-ghetto apartment with the moldy bathroom tiles and my father. Called the airlines and got stuck in a pot hole until I screamed BEREAVEMENT RATE or something equally dramatic and they hopped to it like I was bathed in sepia tones shooting at their heels yelling dance dagnamit dance

Then.

I danced and He danced until my bag was packed buhbye I'll miss you little apartment too bad I don't have plants or I'd tell you to water them while I was gone so you could come into my empty apartment and fill it up a little at a time so it wouldn't be so empty when I came back. But I have no plants because plants and me aren't copacetic you see because I kill them and they DIE.

But even dead plants would be welcome as I said goodbye to the inorganic walls and the plasticmetalwood that I knew I would eventually return to, only much different then. Now was my last time to look upon my refrigerator and my coffee table and the wine bottle covered in dripped wax that my roomate and I had been so giddy over before she fled the coop and my computer that I had gotten such a good deal on and my closet space that is too big for one small person with no money, my last time to gaze upon this dome of wreckage before it became wreckage, the last time to see these objects in the BEFORE and not the AFTER, the fat and not the skinny, which began right now.

THEMES: FAMILY, ANGER, LOSS

Karlaboy
Steven Peros

Play Synopsis: Biographer Bill Lauder has penned a ruthless tell-all about Karla Daven, a long dead legendary 1950's starlet. As a result, he is summoned in the middle of the night to the dilapidated mansion of Karla's husband, Harold Bachman, a reclusive director who claims that Karla's ghost has threatened to kill him this very night unless Bill calls off the publication of his tawdry book of lies.

Character: Karla
Age: 20s
Genre: Dramatic

Scene Synopsis: Karla, in this flashback an emerging film star, wishes she had passion in life like her characters have on the silver screen. She knows how her male audience views her in movies, but longs for romance off the screen with a man who sees beyond her Hollywood image.

Notes:

Karlaboy

KARLA. Haven't you heard, genius? I have every American male wishing he could sleep with me. You know I do. I see it in their eyes. Not just in the street, but right through the lens. I've heard some actresses are uncomfortable with the camera, but not me. It's not some mechanical monster to me. It's like...some sort of funnel to pour myself through. I know that sounds silly, but that's what it feels like every time you say "Action." I softly bite my lower lip – half a second, it's there and gone – and men fifty rows back feel a tremble in their body. *(a beat)* You talk about "the real Technicolor world"... I don't know...sometimes I wonder if I could ever impress a man in the real world the way I do on that screen. I'm just looking for it to be right, that's all. When the man is looking at me, not some pin-up poster, all perfectly lit and touched up. *(a pause)* I know this sounds crazy, but I want a man to fall in love with everything that's ugly about me; then I'll know he's the right one. You know what I mean?

THEMES: BEAUTY, LONGING, LOVE

My First Time
Ken Davenport

Play Synopsis: *My First Time* features four actors in hysterical and heartbreaking stories about first sexual experiences written by real people. Their stories are silly, sweet, absurd, funny, heterosexual, homosexual, shy, sexy and everything in between.

Character: Woman
Age: 20s-40s
Genre: Dramatic

Scene Synopsis: A young woman recounts her first sexual encounter to the audience.

Notes:

My First Time

WOMAN #2. I had a brother four years younger. He was diagnosed with leukemia and eventually underwent a bone marrow transplant. It was an eight hour drive to the medical center so my parents lowered the back seats of the station wagon and placed a wide mattress for Luke and me to lie on because Luke was not so strong for such a long ride. Luke and I were curled up together under several blankets. Luke confided in me that he never had a relationship that had gone beyond kissing and he was afraid of dying a virgin. I continued to hold Luke in my arms as I came to a decision. When we stopped for McDonalds, I asked that Luke and I be allowed to sit at a table apart and my parents agreed. Luke and I had a discussion of what sex meant in our lives. I wanted Luke to understand that I was making a one time, lifetime exception for him, because it would be very wrong in ordinary circumstances. He made his objections about respect, incest, pregnancy. He was willing to refuse me. I put it to him that if he made the utmost effort to live, I would pay a small enough price if this would motivate him. He accepted. I went to the restroom and removed my bra and panties. I stocked up on paper towels. Most important of all I prayed. We all got into the car for the five hour leg of my trip. I removed my jeans. I lowered his jeans to his knees. We made no motion under the blankets. After a few minutes, I felt Luke's whole body convulse and he let out an almost inaudible short moan and a exhalation. My parents heard it and asked what was going on in back. I said that Luke was sleeping restlessly and must have been dreaming. We got our clothes organized and had twenty minutes of snuggling before the gas station. Luke's transplant took but he did not survive the infections while his immune system was shut down. We were never really privately alone again. That is my story. I have no interest in approval.

Dead Man's Cell Phone
Sarah Ruhl

Play Synopsis: An incessantly ringing cell phone in a quiet café. A stranger at the next table who has had enough. And a dead man – with a lot of loose ends. *Dead Man's Cell Phone* is a work about how we memorialize the dead – and how that remembering changes us.

Character: Jean
Age: 30s
Genre: Dramatic

Scene Synopsis: Jean is holding onto the cell phone of a dead man she never knew in life. She tries to explain to his brother why she feels such an attachment to the device.

Notes:

Dead Man's Cell Phone

JEAN. You know what's funny? I never had a cell phone. I didn't want to always be there, you know. Like if your phone is on you're supposed to be there. Sometimes I like to disappear. But it's like – when everyone has their cell phone on, no one is there. It's like we're all disappearing the more we're there. Last week there was this woman in line at the pharmacy and she was like, "Shit, Shit!" on her cell phone and she kept saying "shit, fuck, you're shitting me, you're fucking shitting me, no fucking way, bitch, if you're shitting me I'll fucking kill you" you know, that kind of thing, and there were all these old people in line and it was like she didn't care if she told her whole life, the worst part of her life, in front of the people in line. It was like – people who are in line at pharmacies must be strangers. By definition. And I thought that was sad.

But when Gordon's phone rang and rang, after he died, I thought his phone was beautiful, like it was the only thing keeping him alive, like as long as people called him he would be alive. That sounds – a little – I know – but all those molecules, in the air, trying to talk to Gordon – and Gordon – he's in the air too – so maybe they all would meet up there, whizzing around – those bits of air – and voices. I'll leave his phone on as long as I live. I'll keep re-charging it. Just in case someone calls. Maybe an old childhood friend. You never know.

THEMES: LIFE, TECHNOLOGY, INTERCONNECTEDNESS

What They Have

Kate Robin

Play Synopsis: Connie and Jonas are a successful industry couple. Their friends Suzanne, a struggling painter, and Matt, a struggling musician, can't afford to fix the roof. But stay tuned because in this funny, poignant and always truthful new play, lives can change in a heartbeat, and things aren't necessarily what they seem.

Character: Connie
Age: 30s
Genre: Dramatic

Scene Synopsis: A year after Connie had to terminate her pregnancy due to fatal complications with the unborn child, she is still suffering from the loss of what she had, with little hope for the future.

Notes:

What They Have

CONNIE. I know there could be hope. One could have hope. Hope may even objectively exist. But I don't have it. I can't. It'll kill me. I've been screwed by hope too many times. And right now, that's all I can see. Hope the humiliator. Hope that change is possible. That this country will ever be anything but an empty brain with two ears. That's how it looks to me. New York and California are like these two organs that hear the truth and between them is this big leering face on top of a greedy tub of lard. God! All the dead children. All those poor beautiful mothers whose sons have been slaughtered for nothing. And they brought it on themselves! They voted for it. Or they didn't vote. I tried! I tried to save their sons! I tried. *(She starts to cry.)* This cocksucking IVF. The embryos are going backward now. They put five of these fuckers in me, and I swear to god, they went the wrong way! They were like running from my uterus. It's like no one wants to be my child. Even my own eggs can't stand me anymore. That's what I've become. An embryo scarer. Uch. The GIFT and the ZIFT. ICSI, DICKSEY, and fucking Cottontail, I've done it all. And it's like every new technology we try makes me less pregnant than the last one.But you don't want to hear about this, trust me. At first you'll feel bad for me, but then, in about ten minutes, I'll be ranting, because I've totally lost my mind, and you'll start thinking maybe I'm a little self-indulgent, what with all the real problems in the world, the war and the famine, I can't expect to have everything, and actually now that you think of it, I have gotten everything I ever wanted (which isn't true, at all, but I know you'll think it), so isn't it only fair that this one thing should evade me? Isn't there really a wonderful spiritual lesson, a character building exercise to be found in all this? And the less compassion I feel from you, the more shrill and intolerable I'll become until you'll move past thoughts like "Why doesn't she just adopt?" to "Maybe it's better she not be a mother actually. Some women really shouldn't, and Connie's always been a bit brittle, ambitious. She's not nurturing at all. Thank God she can't conceive. In fact, her infertility is yet another proof that God does in fact exist and is always making the best decisions for the greater good."

Beachwood Drive
Steven Leigh Morris

Play Synopsis: After being arrested in a sting operation, Nadya, a prostitute from the Ukraine, escapes from the snares of both the Russian Mafia and the Los Angeles Police Department. The mystery of Nadya's disappearance unfolds Rashomon-style, as the story is retold through the eyes of four different people involved both personally and professionally in Nadya's life.

Character: Nadya
Age: 30s
Genre: Dramatic

Scene Synopsis: During an interrogation, Detective Cromwell offers protection and a new start to Nadya in exchange for information on her "boss" Vera. Knowing the deadly consequences of ratting out Vera, Nadya questions the reliabilty of the detective's word.

Notes:

Beachwood Drive

NADYA. Fuck you. Fuck you and your new start. Give me one, give me one good reason why I should trust you. Because you're the police? In this city, there is not one, not one person who ever told me the truth, who didn't back out of a commitment. I'm sorry, but that is my experience. A lawyer I met. She wanted to be my friend. I said okay. I knit sweaters. She wanted a sweater for her baby. Fine, I made her one. I didn't ask anything for it. But she said she would help me with my papers. I didn't ask. She offered. When it's time to file my Green Card application, she's very busy, getting ready to move back to Texas. Okay, one rotten peach, you say. But this happens time after time. You think I didn't try to open a clean business here? You think I didn't try? Imported accessories from Ukraine. Hand crafted jewelry. Very simple, very classy, not folk, but trendy, things that would sell here. I took them to a shopkeeper on Franklin, we talked, we laughed, we told stories, I showed her samples. She told me what was interesting for her, what was not. She placed an order. I said let's make a contract because the rings and broaches have to be sent in from Odessa, she says, oh it's such a small order, I'm good for it, she says. I'm good for it. I spent money on that order, a few hundred dollars, no, not thousands, a small order, but that's not the point. When I call to make the delivery, my phone calls are not returned. When I show up at the shop, she's too busy to see me. What can I do? Take her to court? This is the kind of truth I find in this city, time after time. Any idiot can make it through a crisis, it's the day to day living that kills you. That's from Chekhov. Where I come from, when we break our word, we know the cost. The rules are clear. And so is the cost: A broken bone. A bullet in the throat. In Ukraine we have what you people call justice. You Americans use this word, you talk about it, but you never do anything about it. Our justice is clear. Your justice is a joke.

Kosher Lutherans

William Missouri Downs

Play Synopsis: Hanna and Franklyn, a seemingly perfect couple, desperately want to have a child of their own, and are unable to do so. But then they encounter a God-fearing pregnant girl from Iowa who offers to let the couple adopt her out-of-wedlock baby. Just before the papers are signed, Hanna and Franklyn discover the girl is unaware that they are Jewish. Knowing the revelation could throw a ratchet into the works, the couple pose as Lutherans to appeal to the girl's apparent Midwestern sensibilities. But how far are they willing to go to have a family?

Character: Martha
Age: 30s
Genre: Dramatic

Scene Synopsis: Martha is looking for a change in her life to create stability in a world of chaos and suffering. She explains her decision to become Lutheran to her friend, Hannah.

Notes:

Kosher Lutherans

MARTHA. When my sister lost Isaac, I resolved that I wouldn't allow God to put me through that.... I was there that morning. Was babysitting so that they could finally have a weekend together alone...that wonderful little boy – sleeping so soundly – only he wasn't asleep.... And everything that followed. I promised, I promised myself right then and there that I'd never allow God to hurt me like he hurt my sister. ...Have you ever noticed that everyone you know, without exception, doesn't get what they need. My mother, a good woman, dies when I'm twelve. Ben's mother, I'm not saying anything you can't already vouch for, she's a jerk, and healthy as a horse. Ben's father, a kind man, we should all have such a caring soul in our lives, gone in an instant. My father who won't put on pants to answer the door, alive and kicking. My sister...No, we won't go there again... *(beat)* At first I thought that God had left the receiver off the hook. Then I concluded, after much thought and evidence, that God doesn't micromanage... But now, now I'm convinced, God isn't even a noun.

THEMES: FAITH, JUSTICE, LOVE

Sensitivity
from Truth Be Told

Lisa Soland

Play Synopsis: *Truth Be Told* is a full-length play that consists of eleven, one-person stories shared by a variety of personalities, all focused on getting at the truth.

Character: Michelle
Age: 30s
Genre: Dramatic

Scene Synopsis: Michelle struggles with the loss of a man she started dating, who died suddenly before they had even shared their first kiss.

Notes:

Sensitivity

MICHELLE. I've always had this…sensitivity. *(beat)* When I was a kid, I could pretty much feel what other people were feeling. I could feel it so strongly that my own feelings, what I was feeling, was pretty much put on the back burner. After two disastrous, long term relationships, I decided that I was going to face whatever it was that was keeping me from…living out the life that I was supposed to live. *(beat)* I found this therapist and he was good. And he sat there quiet…mostly, for about two years. Quiet helps. *(beat)*

But anyway, during this time I gathered up the courage to sign up with this online dating service. They set me up with this guy, thirty, I guess, and we met for coffee. That's what you do. You meet for coffee and decide whether or not you want to continue the date from there. Well, we did. And when we walked back to our cars, I remember standing by his SUV and thinking to myself, that he wanted to kiss me. I could feel it. But he didn't. So after a few more minutes we said goodbye and I went home. When I walked in the door, there's this email waiting for me from him, saying how he had wanted to kiss me. And I wrote him back and said, "Well…you should have!" *(beat)* Anyway, it was cute. So a couple of days later, I go on my computer and Steve is online, so I instant message him and say, "Hey, you bum. What are you doing home from work?" And he wrote back, only it's not him. It's his friend and he tells me that Steve was killed in a car accident driving back from Las Vegas. Just like that. Gone. The next few days were weird. I started sensing Steve around me. I could feel him somehow in my chest. My heart, maybe. One day, I'm back in with my therapist and suddenly I feel Steve in the room…this amazingly deep sadness and I see…his SUV rolling over and over and over and I feel all this confusion and… *(She shakes her head and stops.)*

Anyway, instead of ignoring it and trying to continue on with my session, I decide to take a chance and tell my therapist what's going on. He listens, and says says, "Tell him to go away." I looked at my therapist and I said, "Can I do that? Can I really just tell him to go away?" And he said, "Yes, you can." *(beat)* So, I did. And he left. And the pain left. No more sadness. No more tumbling cars. And I've been telling things that hurt to leave ever since.

THEMES: LOSS, FEAR, DEPENDENCE

Anon

Kate Robin

Play Synopsis: *Anon* follows two couples as they cope with sexual addiction. In between scenes with these four characters, ten different women, members of a support group for those involved with individuals with sex addiction issues, tell their stories in monologues that are alternately funny and harrowing...

Character: Trish
Age: 30s
Genre: Dramatic

Scene Synopsis: Trish tells her support group about a little project a therapist once gave her.

Notes:

Anon

TRISH. Like four years ago my therapist told me I had to start manifesting a better sort of man in my life – because it was like I didn't believe there were any. I was like, face facts honey, there's not a million great single guys wandering around just dying to impregnate me. And she said, "you don't need a million. You just need one." But you have to know what you're looking for to be able to find it. So she told me to make a list of everything I wanted in a man, a "My man is…" list, and she said, "don't edit yourself, because you think it's impossible to have everything you want" – because of course, I thought you can't have "sexy" and… "nice" on the same list because they cancel each other out – some qualities just don't show up in the same guy, like "successful" and "considerate." I was scared to put down "funny" for example, even though I really like a funny guy, because it always went hand in hand with "highly neurotic," in my experience. Anyway, she said I could have an A list for qualities that were vital, like, you know, "capable of telling the truth." And a B list for things that were negotiable, like "enjoys my family." I mean, come on, we're looking for a human. And she was like "be specific because this is really powerful. Don't write something like "handsome," write "attractive to me" because it's not like you want a guy who everyone in the world wants to sleep with – it's better if you're the only one who does, right?" So, I made my list and I thought it was really comprehensive and two weeks later, I met Jake. And he totally filled the A list and a lot of the B and I thought, this therapist is a genius. Anyway, last week I looked at this fucking list and I realized there was one thing it never even occurred to me to write down: "likes me." Just "likes me."

Come to the Garden
from The Man in the Gray Suit and Other Plays

Lisa Soland

Play Synopsis: Mourning the loss of her third child, the Wife can no longer find pleasure in things she once loved. Any promises she knew from her past all seem to be broken.

Character: Wife
Age: 30s-40s
Genre: Dramatic

Scene Synopsis: Husband, in an attempt to gently help his wife fight her growing depression, suggests that she come to the garden she once loved. Wife can't face the garden, however, as she struggles with grief.

Notes:

Come to the Garden

WIFE. *(impatiently)* The garden, the garden. I'm tired of looking at it. It tires me. That garden never produces anything. Nothing at all. I work. I slave. And the corn gets knee high by the fourth of July and then it dies. What in the hell is that about? And the tomatoes. So large. So pregnant with promise and then, just before we're to pick them, just before the red is almost perfectly ripe, some deviant, evil thing starts tearing away at it. Small bites at first and the next thing you know it's crawling with something or other and we've lost it. We've lost it. *(She begins to cry.)* All that promise just flushed down the toilet. Flushed down the toilet before it's even got a name. Before we even have time to name it, it's gone. I'm done with it, Honey. I'm done. Three is too many to lose. I'm done. I'm not stepping foot in that fucking garden ever again.

THEMES: FAMILY, DEATH, LOSS

When Is A Clock

Matthew Freeman

Play Synopsis: When Gordon's wife vanishes, the only clue to her whereabouts is a bookmark in dog-eared copy of *Traveling to Montpelier*. With little help to be found at work, from his son, or from the police, Gordon takes off to a rural bookstore to find some answers. Through a fractured narrative that is half-mystery and half-memory, synchronicity, dreams, and alchemy combine in an exploration of what it means to be able to – and unable to – change.

Character: Bronwyn
Age: 30s -40s
Genre: Dramatic

Scene Synopsis: Bronwyn, who has left her husband and son to embark on a new life, recounts one affair she has had from the perspective of becoming a clock. She speaks candidly to the audience.

Notes:

THEMES: SECRECY, SEX, LOVE

When Is A Clock

BRONWYN. I was a clock. This hairy man with red wet eyes put me in a bag and brought me home and put me on his mantle, just above an imitation stone fireplace. His wife saw me and didn't think anything of it. Just one more little thing around the house. I don't know how she could have missed what was happening right in front of her. My wooden doors, my two hands, my little mechanisms whirling, my cherry wood frame...I could see him looking at all the tiny parts as his wife droned on about the price of gasoline. I never felt so... Loved. When he was gone, I'd watch his wife read magazines and masturbate. Then he'd come home and go straight for me, smiling and making sure I was wound. After dinner, when she would wash up, he'd take me and then open up my doors and clean me gently. The first time I was frightened. I mean, I wasn't really a clock, I thought. What if, by opening me up, he'd kill me outright. But, instead of tiny organs, I could see my metal insides in his glasses. It was uncomfortable, the pipe and brush. I felt like I would burst out laughing or crying. But I couldn't get caught, so I settled into it, relaxed into it, for the sake of secrecy. By the third day my mind completely changed and even knew this process as relief.

(pause)

The hard part was leaving him.

God's Ear

Jenny Schwartz

Play Synopsis: Mel and Ted have lost their young son. Now, wherever Ted goes, he meets people with dead sons. And whatever Mel touches falls apart. Mel and Ted try to continue their way through the world, guided by their young daughter Lanie, and the Tooth Fairy and G.I. Joe.

Character: Mel
Age: 40s
Genre: Dramatic

Scene Synopsis: Mel, speaking to Ted, tries to piece together the doctor's diagnosis of her son who's in a coma after a near drowning incident.

Notes:

God's Ear

MEL. He's in a coma.

He's hooked up to a respirator.

He has a pulse.

He has brain damage.

Due to lack of...

Extensive brain damage.

Due to lack of...

His pupils are unreactive,

they said.

He doesn't withdraw from pain,

they said.

The next twenty-four hours are critical.

Or was it crucial?

Or was it critical?

Or was it crucial?

He's in critical condition,

they said.

Survival.

They said.

His chances of survival.

They said,

low.

They said,

the next twenty-four hours are crucial to his chances

of survival,

they said,

lost. They said,

his reflexes are –

lost.

What do you mean he has a pulse?

I said.

Of course he has a pulse,

I said.

They're doing all they can,

they said.

Helping him to breathe.

Providing him with –

Fluids.

Electrolytes.

Nutrients.

They said.

Most children,

they said,

most children who do survive this extent of a

near-drowning,

extent of a,

most children,

they said,

are unable to walk and unable to talk,

and most children –

I told them our son isn't like most children.

He's not.

Is he?

Bulrusher
Eisa Davis

Play Synopsis: In 1955, in the redwood country north of San Francisco, a multiracial girl grows up in a predominantly white town whose residents pepper their speech with the historical dialect of Boontling. Found floating in a basket on the river as an infant, Bulrusher is an orphan with a gift for clairvoyance that makes her feel like a stranger even amongst the strange: the taciturn schoolteacher who adopted her, the madam who runs her brothel with a fierce discipline, the logger with a zest for horses and women, and the guitar-slinging boy who is after Bulrusher's heart. Just when she thought her world might close in on her, she discovers an entirely new sense of self when a black girl from Alabama comes to town.

Character: Schoolch
Age: 40s-50s
Genre: Dramatic

Scene Synopsis: Schoolch took in Bulrusher as an orphaned child many years ago and tried to protect her from the world's corruption. As Bulrusher gets older, she wishes to venture out into the world and Schoolch wants her to remember where she came from, that to which she is bound.

Notes:

Bulrusher

SCHOOLCH. More backtalk? My house, my rules. Break them, and you can leave here. But you won't. How many times do I have to tell you? When you were a baby, when you were just a few days old, your mama sent you down the river, sent you floating down to the brine. Wanted nothing to do with you. But you got yourself caught in some weeds and the Negro Jeans found you, brought you to the brothel tied up in his suede duster. Put you on the pool table and there you were, kicking up the smoky air. You didn't blink or cry under that hanging lamp, you just lay there kicking for your life. Madame, she ain't the kind to take pity, wasn't going to risk her business taking you in. But even if she said she wanted you, she would have had to fight me. I saw you and I felt like you had answered a question. Your eyes, the clay color of your legs, the curly hair on your head – you seemed like family, like mine. That if I had you, I'd be alright. And if you had me, you'd be alright. I knew I could protect you, I knew that you weren't supposed to be alive, that you weren't supposed to belong to me at all and that's why I needed you. That's why you fit. So there's no separating us Bulrusher, we are just like our names, bound to what we do and what's been done to us. Our names are our fates and our proper place. Don't forget that.

THEMES: Family, Dependence, Belonging

Apostasy
Gino DiIorio

Play Synopsis: Sheila Gold, 55, a successful Jewish business-woman suffering from terminal cancer, is spending the end of her life in a comfortable hospice where her only companion is her thirty year old daughter, Rachel. When Sheila becomes fascinated with a late night televangelist, Dr. Julius Strong, and writes to tell him that she will make a sizable donation to his ministry, he flies out to visit her and the two fall in love. But is it true love, or is the good minister just out for Rachel's inheritance?

Character: Sheila
Age: 50s
Genre: Dramatic

Scene Synopsis: Sheila reveals to Julius how she truly feels about "visiting day" in the hospice.

Notes:

Apostasy

SHEILA. My daughter will be here soon, you'll get to meet her. She's a piece of work. She comes by, brings me a new stash of weed to get me through. And my ex husband, Lenny, he used to come visit, but then he stopped.

(Pause. Sheila looks out the window.)

Visiting day. You sit and you see families walking. And they're smiling and laughing and everybody's on their best behavior. If you didn't know any better, you'd never know there was anything wrong. And if you listen to their conversations, you know what people are saying? Nothing. They're not saying anything. You'd think everybody would be in some kind of a hurry to talk about...I don't know, things left undone, or unsaid. I loved our times together, or I don't regret marrying you, or I never liked your noodle kugel, or it always bothered me when you wore your hair that way. I cheated on you once on a business trip. I don't know why, I just did. Think about me when I'm gone. But they don't. No one says anything of any significance, No one mentions the word death. It's almost as if there's a man behind the curtain and he's going to come out and say, Okay, game's up. You can go home now. You passed the test. Whatever. And then everyone goes home and the night falls and this place gets real quiet. And it begins to smell like death again.

THEMES: PRETENSE, FEAR, DEATH

Stain

Tony Glazer

Play Synopsis: *Stain* follows fifteen year-old Thomas through his quickly-crumbling life and the secrets his family tries to keep at bay. In this darkly comic piece about the complexities of family, Thomas is confronted with a choice that will either save or mark him forever.

Character: Theresa
Age: 70s
Genre: Dramatic

Scene Synopsis: Thomas finds out that his biological father is really his grandfather, Samuel, who raped his mother, Julia. He goes to his grandmother, Theresa, to learn more about this man, where Theresa reveals a shocking memory of her own.

Notes:

THEMES: FAMILY, CONFUSION, MEMORY

Stain

THERESA. When he was alive – this was years ago – we had a
mouse problem. We were pretty sure it was just the one mouse
unless they had it worked out in shifts –I'm not sure how mice
plan these things. Samuel, my husband Samuel, decided to buy
a glue trap and set it where we normally saw the little brown
thing creep about. I had heard glue traps were cruel so I was a
little tentative about it but Samuel insisted it was just a rodent
and it had to be done. Anyway, one night, I awoke to hear
this...squeaking sound. I looked for Samuel but he wasn't in
bed, so I put on my robe and followed the squeaking sounds
and I found Samuel in his pajamas hunched over the glue trap
that he had cut open and, with a spoon, very tenderly separating this wide eyed, brown, little mouse from the trap. And
the mouse squeaked and squeaked but Samuel pressed on,
little by little, delicately but firmly freeing this little, helpless
mouse. I sat there and watched him – it seemed like hours.
When he finally got the mouse free, patches of its fur were
stripped away. You could see parts of its skin exposed and raw.
He opened the front door and the mouse very slowly, very
gingerly limped its way out of our house. I watched Samuel
stand there for a while, looking out the open door, watching
the mouse hobble away. I snuck back to the bedroom and he
never mentioned the moment to me. We didn't have a mouse
problem after that – our little friend was either the only one or
word traveled fast. But I never forgot that. I never forgot how
tender and sensitive, how deeply caring he was. That's how
I remember him now: a warm, sensitive, deeply caring man
who was raping our daughter. But you will never be like him. I
know you well enough to know that.

The Trials and Tribulations of a Trailer Trash Housewife
Del Shores

Play Synopsis: Willi is the trailer trash housewife of the title, not necessarily of her own volition. Her abusive husband won't let her get a job, one of her children is dead, and the other is verboten by her husband because he's gay. Her best and only friend, a large black woman who lives next door, worries about her constantly, always concerned that Willi's husband will end up killing her. But when Willi discovers her husband is cheating on her, the tables turn, and all of their lives will be affected forever.

Character: LaSonia
Age: 30s-40s
Genre: Dramatic

Scene Synopsis: LaSonia explains to Willi about the difficulties of an abusive relationship and although LaSonia is eager to give advice towards a better life, she knows from experience that hope doesn't always win.

Notes:

The Trials and Tribulations of a Trailer Trash Housewife

LA SONIA. *(takes her time, calmly)* She was wearin' this hat. A bright red hat. And it was Easter Sunday morning at the Ebanezar Baptist Church. Child, it was a sea of hats. The sistas can wear themselves some hats on Easter Sunday morning. But my baby sister had on the prettiest hat of all – or maybe it was that that hat framed her beautiful face and it just seemed that her red hat was the prettiest. Or maybe I was just partial. We sat together and sang "He Arose" and "At the Cross" and my baby sister's favorite "Victory in Jesus." *(singing)* "Oh victory in Jesus, my savior for…" Yes ma'am, we sang to the top of our lungs and we felt happy. My people can sing, Willi baby, they sure 'nough can sing. But after we sang, in the middle of the sermon, I looked down – and peaking out from under her long-sleeve red Easter dress – she always wore red dresses – I saw the bruises. And I reached down and ever so gently lifted the sleeve and there were the bruises. The bruises were everywhere. I knew. I knew exactly what was happening and I vowed to Jesus that Easter Sunday morning in a pew at the Ebanezar Baptist Church that I was going to go over the next morning and we were going to pack her up and she was going to leave that poor excuse for a man. And I did. I gave her the LaSonia "what for" speech and my beautiful baby sister listened to me and we did it. Packed up all her things and we had ourselves a plan. See, we knew if we just left, he'd come find her. Bring her back. She had done tried that before. But, if she told him she was leavin' with all her stuff packed up sittin' there, we knew he'd go crazy, start in on her – and that was part of our plan. But timin' was crucial. When she heard him drive up, she was s'pose to call the police, then hang up and call me. The police would show up in the middle of the storm, arrest that bastard, then I would swoop on in for the rescue. It was a good plan, Willi baby. But… *(chokes up)* …she never did call the cops – or me. I don't know what happened. Maybe she didn't hear him drive up. I don't know. I don't know what happened. When they called me to identify her body, her beautiful face was so bashed in we couldn't even give her a proper viewing. We sang her favorite song, "Victory In Jesus" at her funeral – but there was no victory in nobody, Willi. Just defeat. I lost my baby sister, Willi. That's the last time I went to church because I thought – If God allowed this to happen – if this was "His will" like Brother Johnson preached at my sister's funeral, then I didn't want no part – *(She can't continue. Tears tumble down her face.)* And I heard y'all fighin' last night. Then silence. Just silence. And I sat over there scared outta my ever' lovin' mind wantin' to come and check on you, but scared to interfere because last time I interfered – Now you know why I needed to tell you about my sister.

THEMES: FAMILY, FEAR, FEMALE

AUTHOR INDEX

THEMATIC INDEX

OTHER TITLES AVAILABLE FROM SAMUEL FRENCH

EXCEPTIONAL MONOLOGUES 1
FOR MEN AND WOMEN

In an effort to foster awareness of new plays, and provide for the ever-constant need of audition material, we are proud to announce a new series of monologue books highlighting the latest Samuel French publications. Each year, starting with 2008, monologues from or most recent publications will be selected by our editorial staff to be included in that year's collection. Complete with play synopses, a thematic index, and broad range of styles, you are sure to find one that suits your audition needs. A wonderful way to sample our latest publications, too! *Exceptional Monologues 1* includes such titles and authors as: *Eurydice* by Sarah Ruhl, *The Receptionist* by Adam Bock, *In the Continuum* by Danai Gurira & Nikkole Salter, *Bach at Leipzig* by Itamar Moses, and many more.

Contains monologues from:

Additional Particulars by Ed Simpson
All Aboard the Marriage Hearse
by Matt Morillo
Angry Young Women in Low-Rise Jeans with High-Class Issues by Matt Morillo
Bach at Leipzig by Itamar Moses
Baggage by Sam Bobrick
Barrio Hollywood by Elaine Romero
Billboard by Michael Vukadinovich
Callback by Bill Svanoe
Circuitry by Andrew Barrett
Collective Dating by VB Leghorn
Dead City by Sheila Callaghan
The Drunken City by Adam Bock
Election Day by Josh Tobiessen
Eurydice by Sarah Ruhl
Everythings Turning into Beautiful by Seth Zvi Rosenfeld
A Feminine Ending by Sarah Treem
A Fish Story by Jon Tuttle
From Up Here by Liz Flahive
Getting Sara Married by Sam Bobrick
girl. by Megan Mostyn-Brown
Half and Half by James Sherman
Hat Tricks by Dori Appel
I Used to Write on Walls
by Bekah Brunstetter
The Idiot Box by Michael Elyanow
The Iliad, The Odyssey and All of Greek Mythology in 99 Minutes or Less
by Jay Hopkins and John Hunter

In the Continuum by Danai Gurira and Nikkole Salter
Jerome Bixby's The Man From Earth by Richard Schenkman
Kickass Plays for Women by Jane Shepard
Last Chance Romance by Sam Bobrick
Lizards... by Megan Mostyn-Brown
Lobelia Lodge by B.J. Burton
Messiah on the Frigidaire
by John Culbertson
Nest by Bathsheba Doran
New York by David Rimmer
Night at the Nutcracker by Billy Van Zandt and Jane Milmore
Oldest Living Confederate Widow: Her Confession by Allan Gurganus and Jane Holding
Our Leading Lady by Charles Busch
Outrage by Itamar Moses
The Receptionist by Adam Bock
Rose Colored Glass by Susan Bigelow and Janice Goldberg
Sealed for Freshness by Doug Stone
Smoke and Mirrors by Joseph Goodrich
The Sunken Living Room by David Caudle
The Three Musketeers by Ken Ludwig
Treasure Island by Ken Ludwig
Truth and Reconciliation by Etan Frankel
Trying by Joanna McClelland Glass
Who Killed the Sausage King?
by Roger Karshner

SAMUELFRENCH.COM

OTHER MONOLOGUE COLLECTIONS AVAILABLE FROM SAMUEL FRENCH

All's Well That Ends Swell
50 Fabulous Classical Monologues for Men
50 Fabulous Classical Monologues for Women
Both Sides of the Story
Next!
His & Hers
Actors Write for Actors
Going Solo
Listen to This
Encore!
Two Minutes to Shine, Volumes 1-5

଼ଠଓଔ

SAMUELFRENCH.COM